MW00452998

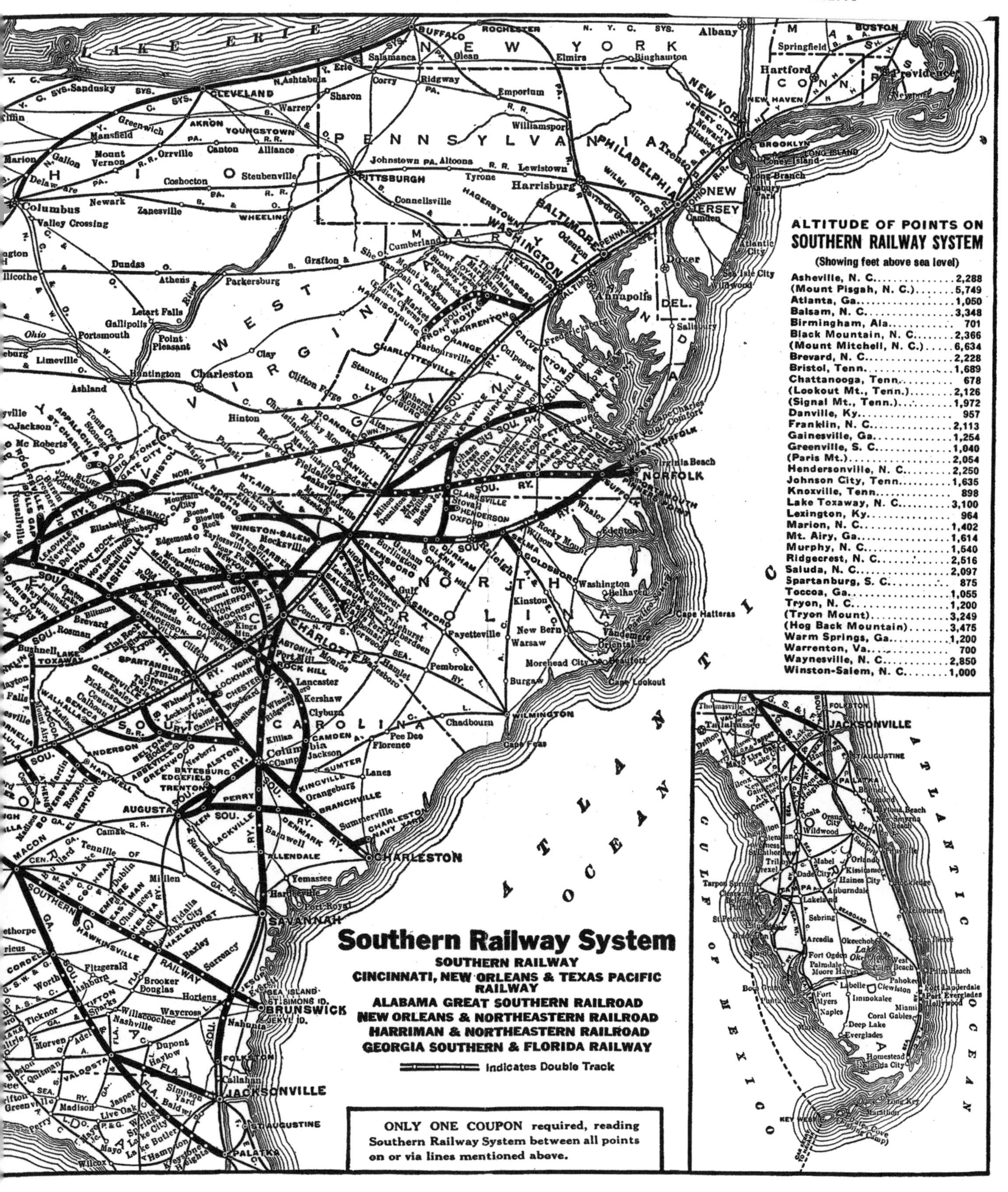
ALTITUDE OF POINTS ON SOUTHERN RAILWAY SYSTEM
(Showing feet above sea level)
Asheville, N. C. 2,288
(Mount Pisgah, N. C.) 5,749
Atlanta, Ga. 1,050
Balsam, N. C. 3,348
Birmingham, Ala. 701
Black Mountain, N. C. 2,366
(Mount Mitchell, N. C.) 6,634
Brevard, N. C. 2,228
Bristol, Tenn. 1,689
Chattanooga, Tenn. 678
(Lookout Mt., Tenn.) 2,126
(Signal Mt., Tenn.) 1,972
Danville, Ky. 957
Franklin, N. C. 2,113
Gainesville, Ga. 1,254
Greenville, S. C. 1,040
(Paris Mt.) 2,054
Hendersonville, N. C. 2,250
Johnson City, Tenn. 1,635
Knoxville, Tenn. 898
Lake Toxaway, N. C. 3,100
Lexington, Ky. 964
Marion, N. C. 1,402
Mt. Airy, Ga. 1,614
Murphy, N. C. 1,540
Ridgecrest, N. C. 2,516
Saluda, N. C. 2,097
Spartanburg, S. C. 875
Toccoa, Ga. 1,055
Tryon, N. C. 1,200
(Tryon Mount) 3,249
(Hog Back Mountain) 3,475
Warm Springs, Ga. 1,200
Warrenton, Va. 700
Waynesville, N. C. 2,850
Winston-Salem, N. C. 1,000
Southern Railway System
SOUTHERN RAILWAY
CINCINNATI, NEW ORLEANS & TEXAS PACIFIC RAILWAY
ALABAMA GREAT SOUTHERN RAILROAD
NEW ORLEANS & NORTHEASTERN RAILROAD
HARRIMAN & NORTHEASTERN RAILROAD
GEORGIA SOUTHERN & FLORIDA RAILWAY
Indicates Double Track
ONLY ONE COUPON required, reading Southern Railway System between all points on or via lines mentioned above.
LAKE ERIE
NEW YORK
PENNSYLVANIA
OHIO
WEST VIRGINIA
VIRGINIA
NORTH CAROLINA
SOUTH CAROLINA
ATLANTIC OCEAN
GULF OF MEXICO
PITTSBURGH
CLEVELAND
BALTIMORE
WASHINGTON
PHILADELPHIA
NORFOLK
CHARLOTTE
CHARLESTON
SAVANNAH
BRUNSWICK
JACKSONVILLE
WILMINGTON
AUGUSTA

# Southern Railway Steam Powered Freight Trains — In Action

By:
Curt Tillotson, Jr.

## *Volume II*

2005 • TLC Publishing Inc. • 18292 Forest Road • Forest, VA 24551

# Table of Contents

I. Dedication ....ii
II. Acknowledgements ....iii
III. Introduction ....iv
IV. Steam & Spencer = A Railfan's Paradise ....1
V. Switchers: 0-6-0's & 0-8-0's ....6
VI. Consolidations: 2-8-0's ....11
VII. Light Mikados: 2-8-2's ....19
VIII. Ms-4 class Heavy Mikados: 2-8-2's ....28
IX. The powerful Santa Fe's: 2-10-2's ....68
X. The massive 2-8-8-2's ....71
XI. Mountain Railroading:
A. Mighty Saluda Grade ....81
B. The "Swannanoa Route" ....99
XII. Bibliography ....107

# Dedication

This book is dedicated to the two people I will ever love the most in my entire life and they were my best friends as well: my parents (Mr. & Mrs. Curtis C. and Alfreda Tillotson). I feel that I am a very lucky person since I had these two kind, gentle and understanding individuals as my Mom and Dad.

To the photographers who were at track side photographing Southern's magnificent steam power in action, you have both my deepest respect and admiration for capturing the past on film so that the current and future generations of railfans can see just how it truly was during the wonderful and dramatic Steam era. Thank you, my old friends!



ISBN 0-9766201-5-4

Front Cover:

Top Left: No. 5021, one of Southern's class Ss-class 2-10-2s assaulthing the famous 4.79% Saluda Grade in March 1952 (see page 83). *(Wayne Brumbaugh)*

Bottom Right: With a trail of exhaust, Ls-2 class 2-8-8-2 Articulated No. 4053 is seen pulling 65 cars of peaches at 55 mph near Chattahoochee, Ga. on August 25, 1946 (see page 76). *(R. D. Sharpless)*

Layout and Design by Christine Howard and Heather Kirk
of Graphics By Heather, Lynchburg, Virginia
www.GraphicsByHeather.com

Printed by Walworth Publishing Co., Marceline, MO 64658

# Acknowledgments

During the last 45+ years, I have been photographing trains. The vast majority of my work covered the Southern Railway System. Why the Southern? Two of my uncles were engineers for the Southern. My grandfather was a Southern track section foreman. The Southern's East Durham, N.C. to Keysville, Va., part of their Richmond Division, passes in front of my home. As a young man, I grew up with the attractive Southern Consolidations (2-8-0's) which controlled "my" line. My old "friends" were: No. 319, 385, 390, 391, 400, 401 and 402 — the most handsome 2-8-0's of any railroad!

During the ensuing years, I must have taken between 14,000 and 15,000 negatives of many roads such as the SAL, SCL (and all the other names until the creation of the current CSX), the N&W, ACL, P&N, A&D (NF&D), etc. However, at least 10,000 of my exposures covered the Southern from 1959 until its merger with the N&W on June 1, 1982; now I follow the current Norfolk Southern Corp.

At the same time I was making exposures of rail action, I also started collecting 8 x 10 enlargements of the Southern during the steam era since most of my childhood was spent watching and admiring the beautiful, colorful Ps-4's, Ps-2's as well as the impressive Ms-4 heavy Mikados and, of course, my 2-8-0 "friends." I knew that many of these lucky photographers who made exposures of these "human-like" machines, while I just watched the action, would eventually be in that big "roundhouse in the sky," so I collected as many enlargements-especially action shots-of this road that "served the South."

I must have nearly 2,000 of these historic photos. As a result, I want others to share in the excitement which I experienced during my childhood and most of my early teen years, watching these clean, colorful locomotives in action, so you can (hopefully) have an idea of those wonder years of my youth, seeing those Southern steam locomotives alive and the main motive power used to help our nation grow and prosper, even during those scary times of World War II when the nation's railroads were called upon to do the almost impossible task of moving men and their war machines and goods. Indeed, the rails carried 95% of the soldiers and their war material.

The only good thing to come out of the war years other than the free world's conquest of the dictators, was to extend the life of the steam locomotive since just before the war began, the Southern and other farsighted roads knew the future of America's railroads would be with the diesel-electric locomotives.

Listed in this article are those photographers and/or collectors who had steam action photos of this innovative and financially successful plus, "railfan friendly," road who helped me collect these example of railroads at a time when the world moved at a slower pace and the "iron horse" was the major form of motive power for practically all trains.

These photos helped me to increase my admiration and respect for the Southern and their stable of the most attractive, well-kept, colorful and beloved steam locomotives in action – not in excursion service – but the rail's major form of engines to move their trains. To these dedicated individuals, I have nothing but admiration and envy: Frank Ardrey, Jr., Wayne Brumbaug, H. Stafford Bryant, Jr., Wiley Bryan, Ray Carneal, Frank Clodfelter, David Driscoll, Dan Finfrock, Doyle Inman, John Krause, Shelby Lowe, L. A. McLean, C. K. March, Bruce Meyer, Richard Prince, David W. Salter, R. D. Sharpless, Southern Railway's Publicity Dept., August A. Thieme, Jr., Walt Thrall, Harold Vollrath and C. W. Witbeck.

*Curt Tillotson, Jr.*

# Introduction

During the late 1890's, our country suffered during an economic depression which affected all parts of society and businesses.

The railroads were so adversely hurt by those hard economic times that many went bankrupt as a result of the loss of business. Southern railroads were especially hard hit since many had not completely recovered from the effects of the War Between the States (1861-1865).

Even though the railroads were suffering from the economic disaster, many bankers and investors in general knew that railroads were still a wise investment. And with the hard times, they could make some of their purchases at rock bottom prices.

The House of (J. P.) Morgan, one of the largest banking interests in New York City, decided to take advantage of these negative circumstances. They were interested in two of the larger Southern roads: the Richmond & Danville and the East Tennessee & Georgia railroads. On July 1, 1894, the two roads were combined into one company known as the Southern Railway System. One of Morgan's most successful "trouble shooters" and respected businessmen, Samuel Spencer, became the first president of the new railroad (and remained so until 1906). Under his leadership, the Southern prospered and began a rapid expansion program which added dozens of other roads to the Southern family. Indeed, by the time of the Southern and Norfolk & Western's merger on June 1, 1982 — which created the current Norfolk Southern Corp. — the Southern consisted of 10,200 miles of railroad.

When the Southern began operations in 1894, the roads it had acquired consisted of mostly antiquated motive power, rolling stock and tracks were in need of extensive repairs. The motive power consisted mostly of Moguls (2-6-0's), Tenwheelers (4-6-0's) and even the ancient American class 4-4-0's.

Shortly after the creation of the Southern, it purchased 173 Consolidation 2-8-0's to help improve the movement of heavier freight traffic at a faster pace. Several hundreds more of the 2-8-0's were obtained over the following years. In fact, the Southern eventually had the largest fleet of 2-8-0's in the South. Then, in 1903, the road's first Pacific type 4-6-2 appeared on their roster. Now the Southern had 2-8-0's pulling a majority of their freights while the 4-6-2's handled the main passenger runs.

By World War I, the steel cars were rapidly replacing those made of wood and business increased dramatically. The 2-8-0's and 4-6-2's began having problems in moving the heavier trains at an acceptable speed. By 1911, the Southern purchased the first of their M-class 2-8-2's. The Mikados proved to be superior to the Consolidations. Then, in 1917, the T-class Mountains (4-8-2's) joined the road's motive power roster. And by 1917-18, the massive Santa Fe type 2-10-2's were used to pull more tonnage at a respectable rate of speed, especially in the road's mountainous territory. At this same time, the huge, power-

*See Page 7 in "0-6-0 & 0-8-0 Switchers"*

ful and impressive 2-8-8-2 articulated "monsters" joined the road and became the most powerful and largest steam locomotives owned by the Southern.

After the Great War, as business continued to increase and the rolling stock grew heavier, two new types of motive power appeared on this progressive road: the heavy Ms-4 class Mikado's 2-8-2's. They proved so successful that the Southern made the Ms-4's the standard main line freight power. In 1923, the renowned and probably the most famous of all Southern's steam power appeared on the road: the beautiful, heavy class Ps-4, Pacific (4-6-2's). They were very attractive engines when they went to work for the road in 1923; however, in 1926, they were painted a most pleasing green and gold and, as the saying goes: the rest was history!

*See Page 103 in "Swannanoa Route"*

By 1923, the Southern finally had the three types of engines that could move the freight and passenger trains the way that met all of the road's requirements: the heavy Ms-4 Mikados handle the freights, the Ps-4 heavy 4-6-2's for their passenger power and the T-class Mountains which handled their varnish assignments in the mountainous areas of the system. These three types of steam power remained the Southern's major engines until the arrival of the diesel-electric locomotives. The lines with light rails and bridges that could not accommodate heavy engines had the 2-8-0's as their main power and the Consolidations could be found handling local freights on the road's main lines as well.

In this book, we will concentrate on the Southern's best 0-6-0 and 0-8-0 switchers, the light and heavy 2-8-2's as well as the light and heavy Pacifics; the 2-10-2's and 2-8-8-2's will be shown in the mountainous terrain around the Asheville, Knoxville and Birmingham areas.

Steam operations on both the scenic yet difficult "Swannanoa Route" and the grueling Saluda Grade — the steepest main line grade in our country which resulted in a 4.7% to 5.01% climb — will be thoroughly covered.

Look at the Southern's magnificent steam freight power in this volume. You will discover the thrilling moments of the steamers taking on the mountains and the fast running on the road's main line territories. You will also discover why the Southern earned a reputation for having the best maintained, cleanest and most appealing engines on any road anywhere (in my opinion).

Hopefully, you will enjoy a look back to a time when steam ruled the rails, a time when these "human-like" locomotives kept a shine on Southern rails and a smile on the faces of all railfans, including yours truly. Enjoy these wonderful days when each approaching steam powered train was an "adventure" to all of those at track side.

*Curt Tillotson, Jr.*

# Steam & Spencer = A Railfan's Paradise

Imagine being able to walk-and photograph-among dozens of steam locomotives-not on the storage or scrap tracks-but active engines ready for assignments, taking your time in viewing the best of the Southern Railway's magnificent fleet of "iron horses." This was a reality in Spencer, N. C. during the late 1940's.

Spencer: if ever there was a true, 100% railroad town, this small community, just north of larger Salisbury, N. C., would rank very high among other areas such as Altoona, Pa., Roanoke, Va. and any other location where railroading was the main occupation of its citizens. Indeed, well over 80% of the inhabitants of this town, this lexicon of railroading which was located approximately halfway between Washington and Atlanta and the end of the mountainous line from Asheville, N. C., were employed by the Southern during the steam era.

Two of the major types of engines used in hauling freight on the Washington-Atlanta main line and the rugged journey to Asheville were found in abundance on the Spencer ready tracks: the esthetically pleasing Ms-4 class heavy 2-8-2-especially those equipped with the efficient Elesco feedwater heater (a majority of railfans ranked these Ms-4's just below the famous Ps-4 heavy Pacifics in the "looks" department) ruled the main line until the arrival of the diesels. The massive and powerful Ss-1 class 2-10-2's were among the major motive power to get freight to and from Asheville.

These and other freight engines: light 2-8-2's, 2-8-0's-not to mention such elegant passenger power as the green and gold colored Ps-4 heavy 4-6-2's, light 4-6-2's as well as the lean, powerful Ts-1 class 4-8-2's were all found in and around Spencer terminal as late as 1948.

In Spencer, where shop crews could disassemble and rebuild steamers with great efficiency, they also inspected, watered, coaled and washed their "charges" so they would be ready for their next job of moving freight and passengers to their destinations. The Southern's reputation of having the most efficient and clean locomotives was most evident when you visited this "magical" vicinity, looking at the beautiful engines which, literally speaking, were handled and respected as if they were members of the Southern's family-each and every class of steam locomotive, both big and small.

The four enlargements included in this section will prove that this reputation was well deserved. I challenge anyone to find engines such as the Ms-4's, the 2-10-2's-especially the magnificent passenger power and even the 2-8-0's and switchers-that operated and looked more pleasing to the eye as those of the Southern.

My first visit to this Mecca of the steam locomotive, as a very young man, proved to be an event I shall never forget. It was a warm, sunny day; however, as we approached Spencer, I noticed cloudy conditions nearly 2-3 miles from and over the town while the remaining areas were bathed in sunshine. Once in Spencer, Mom, Dad and I discovered that they were not normal clouds per se, but it was a cloud-like haze of smoke from a large number of steam locomotives which had created this phenomenon. What an experience: steam engines everywhere-all active, all washed and a majority of them had the rims of their wheels trimmed in white paint (not for excursion duty but for regular service). I found my favorite Elesco feedwater heater equipped Ps-4's and the impressive 2-10-2's and other Southern engines in and around the large roundhouse and ready track areas. Talk about being impressed, I was almost overwhelmed with excitement, joy and sights that made me what I am today: I was a railfan for life!

Now, look at the following photos and imagine that you were with the photographers who made these outstanding and historic exposures during a time when steam was still king on the Southern. As Mr. Spock from the "Star Trek" television series would say: FASCINATING!

It was late afternoon on May 29, 1949, when the photographer made this outstanding exposure. Ironically, he found the two major forms of steam motive power for the Southern's Washington-Atlanta main line (the Ms-4 heavy 2-8-2's) and the rugged, mountainous but beautiful Salisbury to Asheville route (the mighty Ss-1 2-10-2's)-all being prepared for another assignment.

From left-to-right, we find Ms-4's No. 4908 and No. 4886-both equipped with the Elesco feedwater heater. Then we see two "mountain maulers" being readied for another battle with the Blue Ridge Mountains on its way to the "Land of the Sky": No. 5068 and No. 5060-both Ss-1 class 2-10-2 Santa Fe types (named "Santa Fe's" since the Santa Fe was the first railroad to use the 2-10-2 wheel arrangement.)

The Ms-4's produced 59,600 lbs. of tractive effort and were used on freights to Monroe and Alexandria, Va., south to Greenville, S. C. and Atlanta plus, via Greensboro, N. C., to Selma, N. C. and on the ACL-with trackage rights-to Pinners Point, Va. The Ss-1's could muster 69,400 lbs. of tractive effort with 57" drivers and were found lugging tonnage to and from Asheville.

Members of the roundhouse and mechanical departments are shown making final adjustments to "their" engines before they headed to Spencer Yard to pick up their trains and move the tonnage to their destinations with dispatch.

Oh, to be able to walk among such a magnificent scene once more.

*Credit: Photographer, Ray Carneal;*
*Curt Tillotson Collection.*

What a sight "for sore eyes!" Pictured here are six Ms-4 heavy 2-8-2's-all main line power and all in mint condition. At first appearance, one might think these engines were in storage. This would not be the case, for these Mikados had been recently shopped, watered, coaled and cleaned-more evidence to prove the Southern's reputation for having the most cared for, clean locomotives in the rail world, was well earned.

These Ms-4's were actually waiting for their next assignments. For years, the heavy 2-8-2's had been the Southern's major power for the Washington-Atlanta main line and other "big rail" areas. They were so efficient at moving tonnage, you could find these Ms-4's on the main lines, albeit in local freight-work train service, even on the road's eve of complete dieselization, which occurred on June 17, 1953 in Chattanooga, Tenn.

Talk about the extra care given to their engines by the Southern "family," just look at Ms-4 No. 4911, which was equipped with the efficient Elesco feedwater heater-which also enhanced the already handsome lines of these 2-8-2's. It was as clean as even the road's green and gold colored, elegant Ps-4 heavy 4-6-2 passenger power. In fact, most railfans ranked these Mikados just slightly below that of the Ps-4 when it came to the esthetically pleasing looks they created: shiny black engine, gold lettering and numbers, white colored rims on the wheels, the running boards, cowcatchers and its immaculate tender-magnificent!

Yes, the Southern crews knew how to care for their steam power. This is one of the reasons that helps to explain how the road's fleet of steamers lasted so long. Don't forget, the newest steam engine purchased by the Southern was in 1928. The date of this exposure was June 9, 1949, and all the locomotives captured on film (No. 4911, 4863, 4856, etc.) looked far better than when they were purchased from Baldwin and Richmond (Alco) years before.

There is an old saying: "You take care of it and it will take care of you." This was truly the case of the Southern's fleet of steam powered locomotives!

*Credit: Photographer, Unknown; Curt Tillotson Collection.*

Spencer: This was where the action could be found in the late 1940's. It was a sunny Oct. 6, 1949, but with so many steam locomotives located in the same area, there was a perpetual haze of smoke surrounding the terminal.

Two popular Ms-4 heavy 2-8-2's can be found on one of the ready tracks. From left-to-right, No. 4805 had been fueled and cleaned; it was scheduled to move tonnage north on the Southern's Washington-Atlanta main line. No. 4826 would soon move to Spencer Yard, get its train and then head to Greensboro, N. C. where it would leave the main line and travel east to Selma, N. C. Eventually, the big 2-8-2 would power a train from Selma to Pinners Point, Va. over the Atlantic Coast Line on which the Southern had trackage rights.

The Ps-4, No. 1374, seen on the right, had just completed a run and was due to be inspected, fueled, washed and made ready for another main line passenger assignment.

This was railroading at its best with the famous fleet of Southern's cleaned and well-maintained steam locomotives. Day after day, seven days a week, 52 weeks of the year, this was the type of scene you could always find at Spencer since during the steam era, there were no "shut-downs" for certain holidays. No, the railroad never stopped operations, carrying freight and passengers to their destinations in all types of weather.

By the way, what was that "thing" found on the extreme left of the photo? Someone called it a "diesel," an F-7A, No. 4230. Well, since it must have been an experimental model, we will ignore it and go on looking for additional steam power to see and photograph.

*Credit: Photographer, Ray Carneal; Curt Tillotson Collection.*

Walking around the Spencer area in 1947, especially between the huge roundhouse (seen in the background) and the ready tracks, was like having a pleasant dream that became a wonderful reality. Sure, the vicinity was dirty and smoky; oil, grease and cinders could be found everywhere, and it was smelly as well: it was heaven for a railfan!

From left-to-right, we find a Ks-class 2-8-0 Consolidation (No. 723), two massive Ss-1 class 2-10-2's (No.'s 5078 and 5059) plus an elegant lady, No. 1407, a green and gold colored Ps-4 heavy class Pacific. Since it was nearly 11:00 a.m. this Aug. 24, 1947, many of the engines assigned to the Spencer power pool were out on the Washington-Atlanta main line, the route to Asheville or working in the yard and/or around the Spencer-Salisbury areas.

Just look at that attractive No. 723. I ask you, have you seen such a beautiful, clean 2-8-0? No, it was not "dolled up" for an excursion run. The crews at Spencer Shops had just finished making repairs to the handsome Consolidation; it was then washed and painted. Then it was sent to the ready track location to await its next assignment-to move freight and add more revenue to the coffers of the Southern.

The two 2-10-2's will soon be working freights on the rugged Asheville Division, heading for the "Land of the Sky," while that renowned and magnificent Ps-4 would eventually be on the main line once more, pulling a varnish at 80+ m.p.h. and putting a smile on the many faces of those lucky enough to see her in action once again.

It is still hard to believe the changes that would come to this area once the diesels controlled all train movements; and, eventually, a new, ultra-modern yard would be built a few miles north of this location. Thank goodness, the roundhouse and other facilities were saved when the Southern donated a great deal of the area to the state of North Carolina which turned this historic location into a museum of transportation. As a result, we have our memories, photos, and now a most impressive museum to remind us just how it was when steam powered locomotives kept the shine on Southern rails and a special warm spot in the hearts of all railfans.

*Credit: Photographer, Ray Carneal; Curt Tillotson Collection.*

# 0-6-0 & 0-8-0 Switchers

No. 6039 (As-11 class 0-8-0); drivers: 51"; engine weight: 214,000 lbs.; steam pressure: 190 lbs; tractive effort: 53,500 lbs.; superheated; Baldwin built: 1922; tender weight (loaded with 8,000 gal. of water and 10 tons of coal): 150,200 lbs.; engine & tender length: 69'6 1/2"; engine height: 14'9"; retired: July of 1954 (sold to David J. Joseph).

One of the most ignored steam locomotives, when the railfans were on the prowl for rail action, was the lowly switcher. However, rail officials and employees knew the "little" 0-6-0's and 0-8-0's were a key part in moving all trains (freight and passenger). Ask yourself this question: how was that freight train, doing nearly 60 m.p.h. on the main line, making your heart beat faster as a result of the joy it provided you, come into existence? This "hotshot" would not have moved if it was not for switch engines putting its consist together! Yes, when it comes to successful railroading, the yard engines remain an essential part of this procedure.

Normally confined to the yards, pushing, pulling and sorting cars into trains or taking inbound freights and placing the cars where they should be. The switcher rarely had an opportunity to have its drivers running on the heavy, shiny rails of a main line. This photo shows that, as the old saying goes: never say never, for depicted here was one of the 16 standard heavy switchers assigned to the Southern's CNO&TP district in action. There were 73 of these small wheeled "brutes" purchased by the road and they did a yeoman's job during their years of service.

No. 6039, an As-11 class 0-8-0, is shown using all of its 214,000 lbs. of engine weight and 53,500 lbs. of tractive effort to help this Chattanooga, Tenn. bound freight out of Danville, Ky. this early morning in Aug. of 1941. You don't see the fireman sitting in his usual position. Why? Look at that most impressive volume of smoke shooting skyward! The fireman was making sure that his engine did the job it was assigned (this job was completed with great gusto!).

It might just be me but I get the feeling that No. 6039 was enjoying its romp on the main line.

*Credit: Photographer, Unknown; Curt Tillotson Collection.*

No. 1697 (A-7 class 0-6-0); drivers: 50"; engine weight: 145,000 lbs.; steam pressure, 185 lbs.; tractive effort, 32,710 lbs.; Pittsburgh built: 1904; tender weight (loaded with 4,000 gal. of water and 7 tons of coal): 87,740 lbs.; engine & tender length: 43'4 3/4"; engine height: 14'6 1/2"; retired: Aug. 22, 1952 (scrapped at Haynes-Spartanburg, S. C.).

This enlargement gives us an excellent overhead view of one of the Southern's standard 0-6-0 switchers of which the road purchased 150. These were the heaviest 0-6-0's on the system's roster.

The fireman of No. 1697 seems to be doing a good job of keeping this yard "goat" with ample steam in order to perform its assignment. And the 0-6-0 was shown in its element, i.e., working the yards-in this case it was busy in Atlanta's Inman Yard this hot morning in Aug. of 1941.

Even this "might mite" had the Southern touch: look at the white colored rims of the drivers, the road's symbols, the pleasing lettering and numbers (both printed in gold). Indeed, the Southern's reputation of engine maintenance and cleanliness enabled No. 1697-built in 1904-to continue at work for 48 years! I feel it would be safe to say that the Southern made a wise investment when they purchased the little 0-6-0.

Back in 1941, the Southern's crews-especially those in yard service-were assigned the same engine each and every day, for years. As a result, the engineer and fireman were intimate with their "friend." They knew when things were right and when things were going wrong with their engine: the three became one! This was also the case with a majority of the Southern's road crews in the 1930's and, in some cases, this intimacy with their locomotive continued until the arrival of the diesels.

Only the crew and the yardmaster knew just how many trains were put together by this little, but essential, beauty over four decades.

*Credit: Photographer, Unknown; Curt Tillotson Collection.*

No. 1711 (A-7 class 0-6-0); drivers: 50"; engine weight: 145,000 lbs.; steam pressure: 185 lbs.; tractive effort: 32,710 lbs.; Baldwin built: 1908; tender weight (loaded with 4,000 gal. of water and 7 tons of coal): 87,740 lbs.; engine & tender length: 43'4 3/4"; engine height: 14'6 1/2"; retired: Aug. 1953 (sold to the Baltimore Steel Co.).

The main job of the switch engines was (and remains) working the yards: making up and taking apart outbound and inbound trains. There are other responsibilities requiring the attention of switcher as well.

One of those "other responsibilities" is shown in this photo. A-7 class No. 1711 had to prepare other engines for runs out of the 0-6-0's territory. The location shown in this photo was East Durham, N. C.-found on the Southern's Greensboro-Goldsboro, N. C. route. There was another Southern line serving the area: the East Durham-Oxford-Henderson, N. C.-Keysville, Va. branch of the road's Richmond Division-"my line!"

It's a chilly afternoon on Jan. 20, 1950 near 2:00 p.m., as No. 1711 helps two of the 7 steamers that worked the Keysville route in getting coal and water-in this case, they were Consolidations No. 390 and No. 400 (both H-4 class 2-8-0's). The 0-6-0 is shown pushing both 2-8-0's into the engine house (located to the left, outside this photo) where they would be inspected and any necessary repairs would be made. After all this, both 2-8-0's would be cleaned and made ready for another run. East Durham did not have a turntable but they had a wye. The two 2-8-0's are actually on the east leg of the wye in this photo.

No.'s 319, 385, 390, 391, 400, 401 and 402 worked "my line." Indeed, I grew up with these beauties, watching them work in my hometown of Oxford, seeing them going to and returning from their round trip over the Oxford-Henderson branch and then heading north to Keysville. Usually, the Keysville to East Durham freight passed my area while its northbound counterpart was on the Henderson branch.

I loved all these 2-8-0's; however, No. 400 had a special place in my memories. This was caused by several factors: No. 400 almost always had its driver rims painted white (the "Southern touch"), it was the fastest of the group keeping "my" rails shiny and its "stack talk" seemed to be sharper than its sisters (at least to me).

These little Consolidations made me a railfan even before I started school. The A-7 switchers I found in East Durham were also among the most esthetically pleasing A-7's among all of the 150 owned by the Southern.

I hope "my" Consolidations and the A-7 switchers are still operating in that big "roundhouse in the sky." They are still in this railfan's memories-that's for sure!

*Credit: Photographer, Ray Carneal; Curt Tillotson Collection.*

No. 1650 (A-7 class, 0-6-0); drivers: 50"; engine weight: 145,000 lbs.; steam pressure: 185 lbs.; tractive effort: 32,710 lbs.; Pittsburgh built: 1905; tender weight (loaded with 4,000 gal. of water and 7 tons of coal): 87,740 lbs.; engine & tender length: 43'4 3/4"; engine height: 14'6 1/2"; retired: Oct. of 1949.

If ever there was a classic pose of an engineer and his steed, this is it! With his denim cap, one hand on the throttle and the other gripping a bundle of "waste," leaning forward on the arm rest, urging his engine on, pushing along a cut of freight cars. Bob Butterfield of the NYC's "Twentieth Century Limited" fame, could not have topped this unknown engineer as he occupied the "throne" in the hearts of all railfans: the right side of a clean, hard working steam locomotive.

This was not the cab of a green and gold colored Ps-4 or even a beautiful main line Ms-4 freight mover. Even though No. 1650 was an A-7 class switch engine, it took nothing away from this "king" of the rail world.

The A-7 class locomotive (note "A-7" listed on the cab along with "Atlanta"-the division to which it was assigned) is shown working in Atlanta's Inman Yard on a warm morning in Aug. of 1947. The A-7 was the Southern's standard 0-6-0 switcher and you could find these 150 engines anywhere on the 8,000 miles of the Southern, working in the yards, putting trains together or taking inbound freights and moving their cars to where they should be.

The cab ventilator (on the top) was wide-opened in order to catch any cooling air to help ward off the heat that occupied the cab of this busy and essential 0-6-0. Just look at how clean and well

balanced everything seems to be. This was the trade mark of the Southern which was well renowned for the spick and span, "elbow grease" they lavished on their engines-be they large or small, passenger or freight power. Everything looked so right!

It was the dream of most every boy my age-in the 1940's-to occupy that august seat as this veteran hogger did while doing his duty. And just think: he actually got paid to occupy this position!

*Credit: Photographer, Unknown; Curt Tillotson Collection.*

No. 1689 (A-7 class 0-6-0); drivers: 50"; engine weight: 145,000 lbs.; steam pressure: 185 lbs.; tractive effort: 32,710 lbs.; Pittsburgh built: 1904; tender weight (loaded with 4,000 gal. of water and 7 tons of coal): 87,740 lbs.; engine & tender length: 43"4 3/4"; engine height: 14'6 1/2"; retired: July of 1953 (sold to the Baltimore Steel Co.).

In some locations, Southern switchers not only worked yards but local industries as well, especially if their yards were not very large. This was the case shown here as A-7 class 0-6-0, No. 1689, serviced several businesses in and around High Point, N. C. during an early afternoon in August of 1949.

The High Point-Thomasville area was (and remains) known as the "Furniture Capital of the World." A vast majority of home and office furniture in our nation was made in this part of the "Tarheel State." As a result, a huge volume of raw material arrived in these two communities off the Southern's Washington-Atlanta main line. Then, the finished products were sent to all parts of our country and to several locations overseas. The A-7 class switcher, with its white rimmed drivers, had a great amount of work to do: taking the inbound cars that arrived from the main line and getting them to the proper factories. Then the 0-6-0 took the finished goods from the industries back to the yard, putting them together so that a mainliner could pick up these cars and carry them to their destinations.

The light weight of No. 1689 enabled it to negotiate small rail areas around industrial sidings and then the big rails of the main line as well. Its 32,710 lbs. of tractive effort also gave the "little giant"-the standard 0-6-0 on the Southern-enough "muscle" to do its job in a most efficient and expeditious manner.

No. 1689 entered the Southern's roster in 1904 and remained there until July of 1953-49 years! The Southern really got its money's worth out of this vital but most overlooked steam locomotive. It was not a green and gold colored Ps-4 or Ms-4 freight hauler; however, its role in railroading was just as important as the more famous and photographed main line power.

*Credit: Photographer, John Krause; Curt Tillotson Collection.*

No. 1709 (A-7 class 0-6-0); drivers: 50"; engine weight: 145,000 lbs.; steam pressure: 185 lbs.; tractive effort: 32,710 lbs.; Baldwin built: 1908; tender weight (loaded with 4,000 gal. of water and 7 tons of coal): 87,740 lbs.; engine & tender length: 43'4 3/4"; engine height: 14'6 1/2"; retired: May of 1950.

Here is a Southern A-7 class 0-6-0 switcher "in its element," performing yard duties. In this case, we see No. 1709 at the west end of the East Durham, N. C.'s yard at 2:00 p.m. on Oct. 20, 1948.

Even with the dirt and grime associated with yard work, look at how clean and shiny this yard "goat" appears. This was the Southern's tradition of keeping its motive power-big or small-not only looking good but well maintained as well, over the entire system, be it Atlanta, St. Louis, Alexandria, New Orleans, Spencer or East Durham. The last new engine purchased by the Southern was in 1928. Yet, in all the following years, especially the hectic days during World War II when every engine that could make steam was used to move the unbelievable war tonnage, troops and the general public, the road's motive power remained to be known for their good looks even up to the complete dieselization of the road in 1953.

No. 1709 had to not only work the East Durham yard, it served the factories, especially the tobacco plants, in and around the area. The 0-6-0 also had to move the engines that worked the East Durham to Keysville, Va. line, to enable them to get coaled, watered and inspected. The A-7 had to work the several freights that passed through on the Southern's busy Greensboro-Goldsboro, N. C. line (its rails are seen to the right of No. 1709). Yes, it was hard work but that was precisely what the 0-6-0's and 0-8-0's were designed to do. And the 150 A-7 class 0-6-0's will be remembered for their excellent performance and dependability. No. 1709 worked for the Southern over 42 years. Not many roads could boast of such locomotive longevity. The Southern's "TLC" which they lavished on its steamers really paid off in the long run.

*Credit: Photographer, R. B, Carneal; Curt Tillotson Collection.*

# The 2-8-0 Consolidations

After the formation of the Southern Railway System on July 1, 1894, it inherited numerous types of small and old steam motive power. This collection of "ancient" engines continued as the road expanded, purchasing and/or leasing many other lines.

By the end of the 19th and the beginning of the 20th century, the number one engine in use was the 2-8-0 Consolidation. The older American 4-4-0's, Atlantic 4-4-2's, Mogul 2-6-0's and even the Tenwheeler (4-6-0's) had passed their prime. They could not cope with the heavier rail equipment, the tremendous demands for moving freight and passenger trains faster and, simply put, their time had passed.

The 2-8-0's could do most all that was required of them. Of course, some of the 2-8-0's were lightweight and had low tractive efforts. As a result, in 1903, Southern officials met with mechanical engineers from both Baldwin and the Richmond Locomotive Works and came up with a modern 2-8-0, the K-class Consolidation. This class of 2-8-0 was destined to be the standard main line freight locomotive and the road purchased 400 of the K-class and the even more modern, superheated Ks and Ks-1 through Ks-4's. Only the 2-8-2 Mikados could outperform them. However, many of the 2-8-0's and even older power had to remain in service on some Southern lines due to lightweight bridges and rails, even until the arrival of the diesels. Two such areas included the Meridian, Miss. To New Orleans, La. route as well as the line to St. Louis, Mo. On these and similar lines, the 2-8-0 was the "big" power.

Coming at you, wide-opened, was an H-4 class 2-8-0, No. 400, leaving East Durham, N. C., heading to Oxford, N. C.-where it would make a round trip to Henderson, N. C.-and then on to Keysville, Va., where it made a connection with the Richmond-Danville, Va. line-the progenitor of the Southern Railway System.

The H-1's and H-4's ruled "my" line until replaced by the diesels. And, trying very hard to be impartial, they were the most handsome of the 2-8-0 classes. Over the years in my hometown of Oxford, I had an opportunity to ride in the cab of most all of the 2-8-0's that handle the trains on this segment of the Richmond Division: No. 319, 385, 390, 391, 400, 401 and 402. How was I able to ride in these engines? I forgot to mention that one of my uncles was an engineer who worked the Keysville-East Durham line for many years.

No. 400 is shown heading north on the east leg of the East Durham wye, with local freight No. 68 at 7:00 a.m. on June 20, 1949, with 18 "reefers" and 10 other freight cars. Of all the 2-8-0's that kept the rails in front of my home shiny, No. 400 was my favorite: it almost always had white-colored drives and pony trucks; it was considered the fastest of this group of 2-8-0's and, according to my uncle and his fireman, it was also the easiest running 2-8-0 on the Keysville run.

I would see No. 68 (and 69) as it arrived in Oxford, coming by the impressive depot (my "second home") where it would work three huge tobacco processing plants, a coal yard and deliver a great deal of L-C-L to the station (less than car load) merchandise and express.

These beautiful 2-8-0's started my love of trains, of the Southern; it helped me graduate into becoming a true railfan. I missed them so; but, their appearance, sounds and smells will remain with me until I go to join them in that big "roundhouse in the sky."

No. 400 (H-4 class 2-8-0): drivers: 57"; engine weight: 164,800 lbs.; steam pressure: 200 lbs.; tractive effort: 36,827 lbs.; Baldwin built: 1907; tender weight: (loaded with 7,500 gal. of water and 12 tons of coal): 120,000 lbs.; engine & tender length: 64'1 7/8"; engine height: 14'3"; retired: Aug. of 1954.

*Credit: Photographer, Ray Carneal; Curt Tillotson Collection.*

No. 862 (Ks-1 class 2-8-0); drivers: 57"; engine weight: 199,910 lbs.; steam pressure: 200 lbs.; tractive effort: 46,700 lbs.; superheated; Baldwin built: 1906; tender weight (loaded with 7,500 gal. of water and 12 tons of coal): 147,000 lbs.; engine & tender length: 66'4 7/8"; engine height: 15'1"; retired: Feb. of 1953.

The Southern's branch line from Hendersonville, N. C. to Lake Toxaway, N. C. was once a popular trip for tourists since there were several resort facilities at Lake Toxaway which featured scenic vistas of the surrounding mountains which were breathtaking. Unfortunately, by the time of this exposure (Feb. of 1952) passenger service had ceased. However, freight service remained good for several more years. Indeed, there was a daily freight making a round trip on this segment of the Asheville Division plus a daily ex-Sunday local freight taking a round trip as well.

Hendersonville was located on the Spartanburg, S. C. to Asheville, N. C. main line. This mountain town was approximately 15 miles north of the famous Saluda Grade and witnessed some of the Southern's biggest and most powerful steam locomotives such as the Ss-class 2-10-2's, the massive Ls-1 class 2-8-8-2's and the four passenger trains had the beautiful green and gold colored Ts-1 class 4-8-2's passing through the area.

Even though the heavy and powerful locomotives passed through Hendersonville, only the Consolidations were allowed to make the runs to Lake Toxaway due to light rails and several bridges that could not support the heavy main line power.

One of these 2-8-0's-Ks-1 class, No. 862, was pictured just out of Etowah (10 miles west of Hendersonville) with No. 253 at 8:25 a.m.-this Feb. of 1952, pulling 21 cars on its daily round trip, heading towards Lake Toxaway in a most dramatic fashion.

So many railfans flocked to Saluda Grade to witness and photograph the struggle of steam vs. gravity action; this 42-mile branch was mostly ignored. After viewing this westbound freight fighting the mountains, it was fortunate that a few fans took the time to visit and record the action on this picturesque line while steam was still king. As a point of interest, highway U. S. 64 follows this line from Hendersonville most of the westward way to Lake Toxaway.

*Photographer, Wayne Brumbaugh; Curt Tillotson Collection.*

No. 678 (Ks-class 2-8-0): drivers: 57"; engine weight: 197,750 lbs.; steam pressure: 215 lbs.; tractive effort: 47,000 lbs.; superheated; Baldwin built: 1904; tender weight (loaded with 7,500 gal. of water and 12 1/2 tons of coal): 147,000 lbs.; engine & tender length: 66"4 7/8"; engine height: 15'1"; retired: Oct. of 1947.

During the steam era, many of the rail photographers would only make their exposures during the early morning and late afternoon hours, since the sunlight highlighted the entire engine, especially the drivers and lower parts. Looking at this photo, you will see why those railfans preferred to make their exposures during these time periods for the entire engine shows up well in the afternoon sun.

In this case, we find Southern's Ks-class 2-8-0, No. 678, pulling a southbound local freight out of Macon, Georgia at 3:30 p.m. this warm afternoon in August of 1946, with a great deal of work ahead. It would serve all the locations which were ignored by the through freights. Like the switch engines working the yards, the local freights never received the attention from the railfans as did the hot shot freights and, especially, those green and gold colored engines which powered the passenger trains. And yet, the switchers and "peddler" freights were an integral part in the field of railroading.

Notice both ventilators located on top of No. 678's engine cab were wide-opened in order to get more cooling air into the cab so the engineer and fireman could have some relief since they were both located near the extremely hot boiler which provided the steam that enabled No. 678 to make "good time" with a rather lengthy train.

I understand why the older rail photographers did not want to make pictures of trains between 11:00 a.m. and 2:00 p.m. However, I'm ready to release my camera's shutter anytime of the day, regardless of the location of the sun. After all, if rail action occurs during the "forbidden time period," you can bet I'll "snap away" with my camera, for it was rail action at its best!

*Credit: Photographer, David W. Salter; Curt Tillotson Collection.*

No. 712 (Ks-1 class 2-8-0) & No. 573 (Ks-2 class 2-8-0); drivers: 57" (both); engine weight: (No. 712)-199,910 lbs. & (No. 573): 214,000 lbs; steam pressure: (No. 712): 200 lbs. & (No.573): 175 lbs.; tractive effort: (No. 712): 46,700 lbs. & (No. 573): 46,700 lbs.; superheated (both); Richmond built: No. 712: 1904 & No. 573: 1906; tender weight (loaded with 7,500 gal. of water and 12 tons of coal): 147,000 lbs.; (both); engine & tender length: 66'4 7/8" (both); engine height: 15'1" (both); retired: No. 712-Feb. 23, 1950 (scrapped at Haynes-Spartanburg, S. C.) & No. 573: Jan. of 1950.

This photo helps to explain why so many railfans were drawn to the Southern's rugged, yet wondrous "Murphy branch" during the steam era. You had great railroading, numerous bridges, some of the most spectacular mountain scenery through which this segment of the Asheville Division-115.8 miles-traveled.

None of the usual mountain steam power of the Southern, such as the 2-10-2's and 2-8-8-2's could be used on the Asheville-Murphy, N. C. line due to the light rails and a few bridges which could not support these "heavy weights." As a result, the Consolidations-quite often doubleheaded in order to move the tonnage-were the major type of locomotive to rule the "branch." Even the two passenger trains (at the time of this photo-Aug. 23, 1947), No. 17 and No.18, could not use the normal mountain passenger engine: the Ts-class 4-8-2's. Instead, the green and gold colored Ps-2's and other classes of light Pacifics move the public by rail until the discontinuance of passenger runs.

Leaving the Asheville yard and/or passenger station, trains bound for the Murphy branch used the main line to Knoxville, Tenn., crossed over the beautiful French Broad River to Murphy Junction (1.3 miles from Asheville) where they left the main line and headed west, passing through such mountain towns as: Canton, Lake Junaluska, Balsam, Dillsboro, Bryson, Nantahala and on to Murphy. No. 17 took 5 hours to make the 115-mile journey.

Crossing over the Tuckaselee River Bridge near Dillsboro, N. C., an eastbound freight, surrounded by mountains, comes through a deep cut after passing through the Cowee Tunnel, both engines sanding heavily to prevent a loss of traction, as it rumbles on to Asheville. No. 712, a Ks-1 class 2-8-0, No. 573, a Ks-2 class Consolidation-doubleheading-are shown at 10:30 a.m. this hot morning in 1947, at approximately 15 m.p.h. with 31 cars in tow.

The Asheville, N. C. maintenance crews took great care of all their engines, using a judicious amount of white paint for stripping their engines, painting the driver rims, running boards, cylinders heads; the lettering and numbers were in gold colors and the "hogs"-big and small-were washed after almost every run. Even though all Southern division took great pride in the appearance and performance of their engines, the "boys" around Asheville always seemed to do "a little bit more" in their locomotive's "looks." As a result, the Consolidations of the Murphy line were among the most attractive of their wheel arrangement over the entire system.

What a great photo. We can see this wonderful drama without having to endure the heat, humidity, the gnats, chiggers, snakes and the obstacles facing the photographer who put this scene of film so other railfans could experience his "adventure" for years to come. Thank you, Mr. Salter, and "well done!"

*Credit: Photographer, David W. Salter; Curt Tillotson Collection.*

No. 714 (Ks-class, 2-8-0); drivers: 57"; engine weight: 197,750 lbs.; steam pressure: 215 lbs.; tractive effort: 47,000 lbs.; superheated; Richmond built: 1904; tender weight (loaded with 7,500 gal. of water and 12 tons of coal): 147,000 lbs.; engine & tender length: 66'4 7/8"; engine height: 15'1"; retired: Dec. of 1948.

During the steam era, several Southern branch lines could not accommodate larger motive power due to weight and other restrictions. This was also true even on a few portions of the road's main lines and remained so until the arrival of the diesel-electrics.

One example of these restrictions was the NO&NE's (New Orleans & Northeastern) portion of the run between Meridian, Miss. And New Orleans, La.-part of the Southern's Washington-New Orleans route. Another example of the problem(s) was the road's main stem to and from St. Louis, Mo.

The Meridian-New Orleans and Danville, Ky.-St. Louis lines never saw Ms-4 class heavy 2-8-2's-Southern's main freight power-or the Ps-4 heavy Pacifics which were the major mover of passenger trains. Both important segments of the Southern's system had to rely on the 2-8-0 Consolidations and Ps-2 class light Pacifics to move their freight and passenger runs, respectively.

Another example of this dilemma is depicted here in this exposure of Ks-class 2-8-0, No. 714, making good time this early morning in Aug. of 1940, leading 32 cars near Louisville, Ky. The track looks to be in excellent condition with a judicious amount of rock ballast whose edge was "straight as a ruler." From this view, it would appear that bigger motive power could be found. However, there were several bridges and tunnels that could not withstand the bigger steam power's weight and size. As a result, lines such as the runs from St. Louis were among the first to dieselize. In fact, the NO&NE's Meridian-New Orleans route was actually the first divisions on the Southern to completely dieselize.

Today's main lines-all of them-have been rebuilt and any and all weight and other limitations have been removed. As a result, the St. Louis line-a very important portion of the current Norfolk Southern-sees far more trains than when this photo was made and they are moved by the mighty SD-70's, D9-40 CW's and similar diesel "giants."

Still, looking at No. 714, with the fireman really doing his job, made a spectacular moment in rail history, with its plume of smoke shooting skyward, the white-capped engineer leaning out of his cab in a classic pose as he takes this rather long train for a 2-8-0 eastward at a good 35-40 m.p.h. on good track and a great railroad during a time when railroading meant that both freight and passenger trains were moved by the most "human-like" machine ever built by man: the magnificent steam locomotive!

*Credit: Photographer, Collection of Bruce Meyer; Curt Tillotson Collection.*

No. 836 (Ks-class 2-8-0); drivers: 57"; engine weight: 197,750 lbs.; steam pressure: 215 lbs.; tractive effort: 47,000 lbs.; superheated; Baldwin built: 1906; tender weight (loaded with 7,500 gal. of water and 12 tons of coal): 147,000 lbs.; engine & tender length: 66'4 7/8"; engine height: 15'1"; retired: June 1, 1950 (scrapped at Haynes-Spartanburg, S. C.).

Here is a train that railroaders-even railrans-would prefer not to see, for its appearance meant that trouble-serious trouble-had occurred "up the line." Railroaders called it the "Big Hook." It was a work train, on call twenty-four hours every day, that went to an accident so bad that it could not be fixed at the location where a possible derailment, or worse, had occurred. The incident was so serious that it would require the massive and powerful railroad crane, i.e., the "Big Hook," in order to reopen the line so rail traffic could resume.

This July 4, 1947, the extra, headed by Ks-class 2-8-0, No. 836, moves the extra westbound near Chattahoochee, Ga. The extra had all the equipment needed in order to clean up the "mess:" extra track panels, extra rails, ties, spikes, heavy duty jacks and other essential items, along with a crew that had experience in these matters.

Some railfans make exposures of wrecks, derailments, etc.; however, I am not one that was fascinated by such happenings since it meant great destruction of rolling stock, locomotives and, as the modern expression goes "collateral damage"-not to mention the possibility of death.

The 2-8-0 powering the "Big Hook" had graphite on its smoke box, white rim wheels, a clean engine jacket and tender with the lettering and number in gold colors. On the Southern, even the work train's motive power had to meet the road's high standards of appearance and operational efficiency. This was the Southern's way of doing things during the steam era-a reputation that was admired by all, including other railroads.

It was an excellent photograph; however, the significance of this train takes a great deal of the enjoyment away from what should have been a pleasurable event.

*Credit: Photographer, R. D. Sharpless; Curt Tillotson Collection.*

No. 795 (Ks-class 2-8-0); drivers: 57"; engine weight: 197,750 lbs.; steam pressure: 215 lbs.; tractive effort: 47,000 lbs.; superheated; Baldwin built: 1910; tender weight (loaded with 7,500 gal. of water and 12 tons of coal): 147,000 lbs.; engine & tender length: 66'4 7/8"; engine height: 15'1"; retired: March 4, 1952 (sold to the Baltimore Steel Co.).

A local freight acting like a "hot shot" main line through freight could mean one of two things: a first class train was "on its tail" and the local was running as fast as it could to a pass track so it could clear up and not delay the main liner; or it must be a Saturday. An old yardmaster once told me that on a Saturday, the fastest train on the railroad was a local freight, for the crew wanted to reach its destination as soon as possible, mark-off duty and enjoy as much of the weekend as possible!

I'm not sure which reason caused this local to be running as fast as its 57" drivers could make, but it sure created a most dramatic image for the photographer at track-side who made this excellent photo.

Extra 795 South was making good time on the Chattanooga, Tenn.-Atlanta, Ga. main line near Mableton, Ga. this beautiful early afternoon on March 12, 1949, with Ks-class Consolidation, No. 795, proving the motive power, pulling 5 cars and its caboose to home base. The 1910 built 2-8-0 did not show its age which, by 1949, was already 39 years old; but with the Southern's reputation for engine care and appearance, it could help to explain why this "old timer" was acting like a "youngster."

Even though a local freight crew had a great deal of work to do on its main line run, they also had several chances to rest and enjoy the passage of through freights and passenger trains whizzing by. The crew knew all of its customers and what they needed. Indeed, to the individual shipper, the local WAS the Southern Railway System up close, so the crew always went out of their way to please each and every customer. Why? They were employees of the Southern and proud of their road and their train. They provided the best "pr" (public relations) the Southern could ever hope for. Pride in one's company could be an awesome advantage for the road that "served the South."

*Credit: Photographer, R. D. Sharpless; Curt Tillotson Collection.*

No. 701 (Ks-class 2-8-0); drivers: 57"; engine weight: 197,750 lbs.; steam pressure: 215 lbs.; tractive effort: 47,000 lbs.; superheated; Richmond built: 1904; tender weight ( loaded with 7,500 gal. of water and 12 tons of coal): 147,000 lbs.; engine & tender length: 66'4 7/8"; engine height: 15'1"; retired: Nov. of 1952 (sold to the Baltimore Steel Co.).

With only 23 miles from "home," which was Atlanta's Inman Yard, the crew-at least the engineer-appeared tired but happy. This Extra 701 South, with a clear stack and 12 cars plus the "crummy," had been working the busy Chattanooga-Atlanta main line this late afternoon in Feb. of 1942, near Powder Springs, Ga.-crossing over the Sweetwater Trestle.

The Ks-class 2-8-0 proved to be excellent engines in handling local freights, after they were removed from main line service by the more powerful Mikados, especially the Ms-4 class 2-8-2's which eventually became the Southern's standard main line motive power and remained so until they were replaced by the diesels.

The Southern had hundreds of the 2-8-0 Consolidations. Some of the 2-8-0's were light in both engine weight and tractive effort, such as the G-class whose engines only weighed an unimpressive 110,700 lbs.; and tractive effort of only 22,848 lbs., and then there were the mighty Ks-3 class whose engines weighed 246,000 lbs. and they produced a tractive effort of 54,200 lbs.-more than some of the Ms-class 2-8-2's! However, the 400 K-class Consolidations seemed to be the most versatile in both weight and tractive effort.

Many branch lines could only accommodate the light 2-8-0's due to numerous weight restrictions. In fact, most of these branches were the areas once ruled by the Southern's most ancient Tenwheelers and Moguls. And the biggest, most powerful 2-8-0's proved to be excellent motive power in coal country, moving heavy trains of this "black gold" out of the mountains.

No. 701 will soon be in Atlanta where it would take a ride on the turntable, inspected, fueled, cleaned and made ready to head back north on the main line with the same crew that brought it in the day before.

A great number of Southern's Consolidations remained in service until the road completely dieselized in 1953. They were truly versatile engines and most classes of the 2-8-0's were quite handsome in appearance as well.

*Credit: Photographer, R. D. Sharpless; Curt Tillotson Collection.*

No. 753 (Ks-class 2-8-0); drivers: 57"; engine weight: 197,750 lbs.; steam pressure: 215 lbs.; tractive effort: 47,000 lbs.; superheated; Richmond built: 1905; tender weight (loaded with 7,500 gal. of water and 12 tons of coal): 147,000 lbs.; engine & tender length: 66'4 7/8"; engine height: 15'1"; retired: Nov. of 1952 (sold to the Baltimore Steel Co.).

It's early morning in Atlanta, Ga. this beautiful day in Oct. of 1940. And this was the time most local freights would begin their workday. Local No. 161 — shown departing the Georgia capital city-headed by a handsome Ks-class Consolidation, No. 753, pulling 26 cars-was no exception to this tradition. Working upgrade with a train that was heavier than usual for a 2-8-0, we find the Southern "touch" most prominent: white graphite covered No. 753's smoke box, white trimming was found on its running boards and cylinder heads plus a clean smoke stack, engine jacket and tender. How many other roads would lavish so much care on a Consolidation, especially one assigned to local freight service?

After leaving Atlanta, No. 161 would head down the Southern's main line between Atlanta and Jacksonville, Florida. At McDonough, Ga., the local would leave the main and head southwest to Williamson, Ga. and then on to its destination of Fort Valley, Ga. It was a great distance for a local freight and several industries along the way would require the services from the local, so the crew got as much rest as they could while No. 753 pulled out of the city on "big rail" territory. By the time they reached Fort Valley, the crew would be hot, tired and ready for a good meal and soft bed. However, their efforts would result in happy shippers which, in turn, would increase their trust that they could always rely on the Southern for all their needs-this meant good "pr;" i.e., "public relations," for the road.

By the time of this exposure, No. 753 was already 35 years old and yet, looking at the 2-8-0 in action, you would never believe that the Consolidation had been on the road this long since it looked far more handsome than when it was received from the Alco Richmond plant. The 2-8-0 would remain in service for an additional 12 years after this photo was made! Yes, the Southern got its money's worth out of No. 753 and the huge fleet of 2-8-0's. The road also proved an old adage to be true: you take care of it and it will take care of you!

*Credit: Photographer, Richard Prince; Curt Tillotson Collection.*

# Light Mikados, 2-8-2's

The first 2-8-2, Mikado-type locomotive added to the Southern's roster was in 1911. Built by Baldwin, they were numbered in the 4500 and 4600 series. By the way, the very first "Mike" was No. 4501-an engine with a most fascinating future in excursion service. It was probably the most recognized and beloved 2-8-2 among the tens of thousands of railfans who either rode and/or photographed this green and gold colored, esthetically pleasing 2-8-2 during the wonderful excursion era from the late 1960's to the early 1990's. The first Ms-class 2-8-2's (M-Mikado; s-superheated) were also sent to work on the Southern's CNO&TP and AGS areas as well.

The 2-8-2's were an instant success since their larger boiler-whose extra weight was supported by a pair of built-up trailing trucks-enabled them to produce far more steam and, as a result, more power than the road's popular 2-8-0 Consolidations (which were sent to work on the Southern's branch lines and areas that had weight restrictions). Because of their popularity, the Southern eventually had one of the largest fleet of 2-8-2's in our country, ranging from the light Ms class to the far more powerful, heavy Ms-4 type. Indeed, the Elesco feedwater heater equipped Ms-4's were second only to the road's elegant Ps-4 heavy Pacifics among the most admired Southern steam motive power by the railfans.

Even though the road had Ms-6s and Ms-7s, which were more powerful, the Ms-4's remained the Southern's major freight power until the road became 100% dieselized on June 17, 1953.

No. 4529 (Ms-class 2-8-2): drivers 63"; engine weight 272,900 lbs.; steam pressure, 200 lbs.; tractive effort, 53,900 lbs.; superheated; Baldwin built, 1911; tender weight (loaded with 8,000 gal. of water and 12 tons of coal); 153,000 lbs.; engine & tender length, 77' 7/8"; engine height, 15'1"; retired, Sept. of 1951.

You would be hard pressed to find a more dramatic example of this "all weather form of transportation" in action on film. A heavy snowstorm has enveloped the area as Extra 4529 West is shown departing the Richmond, Va. district heading for Danville, Va., 138 miles to the west, this raw Feb. 8, 1947 morning.

Ms-class 2-8-2, No. 4529, is shown with 31 cars in a weather condition rarely seen by non-railroaders for several good reasons: in a full-blown snowstorm, it would be quite difficult to travel in a storm such as this due to the dangerous icy road conditions; and, at least for me, I would be most hesitant to expose my camera in such adverse weather. I must admit, however, that when I was much younger, I would not hesitate to take a chance making exposures in a snowstorm. I would take my "trusty" umbrella, bracing it on top of my head and then "snapping" off a few photos before returning to my car where I would check to see if any of the wet snow got on my camera-especially the lens.

This westbounder, traveling approximately 25-30 m.p.h. with the engine stoker wide-opened, as was the engineer's throttle, "shotgunning" its way through a storm so intense I doubt if the crew could see very far beyond the front of the hard working "Mike."

This portion of the Richmond Division was the progenitor of the Southern. The Richmond-Danville line was part of the group of railroads used to create the Southern Railway on July 1, 1894. It was also the route taken by the Confederate Government to escape the advancing Union Army during the Civil War in 1865. Indeed, Danville became the 3rd and last capital of the Confederate States of America. As a result, this segment of the Southern was among the most historic parts of this successful railroad.

No doubt Extra 4529 West would reach its destination even under these conditions, which blocked the highways and grounded air travel. And, as you can see, our daring photographer not only got his exposure but made it back to his home as well.

Drama-you want drama? Look at this photo in your dry, warm, comfortable home and just imagine how it must have been like to be at track side plus photographing the train as well. I imagine the crew of No. 4529 wondered: what is that crazy "{s*!!!" guy doing out here in this snow?" He was a railfan which, in some cases, takes a little "craziness" to complete what you want to do!

*Credit: Photographer, August Thieme, Jr.; Curt Tillotson Collection.*

The 2-8-2 Mikado type of locomotive could do it all: move through or local freights, passenger trains (if needed), yard work, etc. You name it and the 2-8-2's could usually do it. This was why the Southern-known for its close scrutiny of any motive power before investing their income in major purchases-eventually had one of the largest fleet of 2-8-2's on their roster of motive power.

In 1911, the Southern obtained their first Mikados, giving them an Ms-class identification. With the trailer trucks under the engine cab, it could accommodate a larger boiler since the trucks could support this extra weight. And a bigger boiler meant more power. This, plus their 63" drivers and 53,900 lbs. of tractive effort, pushed most of the 2-8-0 Consolidations off the main lines.

The Ms types were followed by Ms-1's through Ms-4's plus a few Ms-5's, 6's and Ms-7's. The Ms-5's and 6's were huge 2-10-2 Santa Fe types at one time. The Southern took a few 2-10-2's, removed a pair of drivers and made them "large" Mikados with an impressive tractive effort of 59,900 lbs. However, the Ms-4's became the Southern's standard main line motive power with 59,600 lbs. of pulling power and 63" drivers.

The Ms-4's were the most versatile of the M-class engines and dominated the main lines until the diesels finally pushed all steam off the Southern in 1953.

Shown doing nearly 50 m.p.h. is Ms-class, No. 6272 (formally assigned to the CNO&TP) pulling 65 cars of a southbound freight on the Washington-Atlanta main line near Oglethorpe University, Ga. with that big, melodious sounding steamboat whistle "tied down," heading for Atlanta's Inman Yard (approximately 11 miles to the South) on Oct. 11, 1949.

The crew is taking the train from Greenville, S. C. and will be able to "mark off" for the day within an hour or so. Notice how white the northbound tracks appear as compared to the southbound main occupied by the fast moving No. 6272. There was a slight northbound grade in the area which required heavy sanding by the engines pulling tonnage northbound in order to maintain traction with the rails and keep their trains moving at an acceptable speed on this busy main line.

This was the way the Southern did "its thing" in the days of the steam locomotive. What a wonderful time it must have been to have lived when the Southern was ruled by their magnificent fleet of steam power, especially if you were a railfan.

*Credit: Photographer, L. A. McLean; Curt Tillotson Collection.*

No. 6301 and No. 6288 (Ms-1 class 2-8-2-both): drivers, 63" (both); engine weight, 292,000 lbs. (both); steam pressure, 200 lbs. (both); tractive effort, 54,800 lbs. (both); superheated (both); No. 6301, Richmond built, 1922 and No. 6288, Schenectady built, 1918; tender weight (loaded with 10,000 gal. of water and 16 tons of coal); 185,400 lbs. (both); engine & tender length, 81'11" (both); engine height, 14'11" (both); Hodges trailer trucks (both); retired: No. 6288, April of 1952 (sold to the Baltimore Steel Co.) and No. 6301, July 19, 1953 (sold to the Baltimore Steel Co.).

Find a double-headed, steam powered freight train in action comes close to being at the top of a railfan's wish list (including yours truly). To see two, fire-breathing locomotives, hooked together, pulling a tonnage train, to witness two engine crews working together as closely as well rehearsed actors, to hear the engine's exhaust sounds slipping into and out of sync-this was a rail event that you would never forget.

The action described above is shown in this excellent exposure. By the way, adding to the excitement by having this drama occur on a bridge and hearing the rumble of the steel girders comes close to being too much for a railfan to accept! The only thing missing that would put this entire event at the top of every railfan's dream would be large volumes of smoke rolling out of each engine's stack; however, even without the "Mt. Vesuvius" effect, it remains a great photo of steam power at its best.

Two Southern Ms-1 class 2-8-2's-No. 6301 and No. 6288-are shown south of Ludlow, Ky., fighting the stiff Earlanger Hill on the road's CNO&TP, after leaving Cincinnati, crossing the huge double-track bridge over the Ohio River, on a cold, crisp morning in Nov. of 1937.

The photographer heard the "thunder" of two, hard working steamers several minutes before the rumbling of the bridge started and then two Ms-1's came into view. The firemen were "pros" since they had their engine's steam pressure up to the required 200 lbs. with clear stacks (a scene that would put a smile on the face of a Southern official since it meant the crews were not wasting fuel).

Look at this photo. It depicts a sight you would never see again after 1953 when the Southern completely dieselized its motive power. And just think: this used to be a common sight during steam operation. Remember, in 1949, there were no radio communications between the engine crews. It was simply experience at work coordinating every movement of their 2-8-2 charges in perfect unison. It was, for the time, a photo recording railroading at its best!

*Credit: Photographer, Dan Finfrock Collection; Curt Tillotson Collection.*

No. 4568 (Ms-class 2-8-2): drivers, 63"; engine weight, 272,900 lbs.; steam pressure, 200 lbs.; tractive effort, 53,900 lbs.; superheated; Baldwin built, 1913; tender weight (loaded with 8,000 gal. of water and 12 tons of coal); 153,000 lbs.; engine & tender length, 77' 7/8"; engine height, 15'1"; built-up trailer trucks; retired, May of 1950.

After passing through the community of Pacolet, S. C., the engineer opened his throttle and the Ms-class 2-8-2 responded; and the extra freight gathered speed for the last few miles of this Columbia to Spartanburg, S. C. freight's run. Within 13 miles, this Extra 4568 North would arrive in Spartanburg's Haynes Yard. Once in the yard, its crew would "mark off," completing its 94-mile "adventure."

The Columbia-Spartanburg segment of the Southern's Charleston, S. C. to Cincinnati route was served by four passenger trains at the time of this exposure: No. 9 and 10-the "Skyland Special" (Columbia to Asheville, N. C.) and the historic No. 27 and 28-the "Carolina Special" (Charleston, S. C. to Cincinnati-Chicago). It also accommodated two through freights and a local each way. However, at the busy seaport of Charleston, it was not unusual to see a few extras thrown into the flow of rail traffic. Today, even without passenger service, the Norfolk Southern runs numerous trains over this 132-lbs. ribbon rail route, especially piggbacks carrying numerous automobiles and containers plus coal and general freight movements.

The photographer got lucky since clouds were moving into the area when he made this excellent exposure. With the smoke curling back over the 66-car train, you could tell this handsome 2-8-2 was using its 53,900 lbs. of tractive effort to gather speed. Lines like this: Columbia-Spartanburg, Columbia-Charlotte, Richmond-Danville and other similar areas of the Southern, were territories where you could find the light Mikados as the bigger, more powerful Ms-4 2-8-2's began to dominate in moving tonnage on the busy main lines. They continued to do so until the EMD-built diesels eventually removed the steamers from the road for good in 1953. Still, the 4500's and 4600 series of light 2-8-2's could provide beautiful scenes, just waiting for a rail photographer to record these attractive "Mikes" on film. Indeed, with the graphite-covered smoke box, shiny bell and overall clean appearance (the "Southern touch"), they were attractive motive power, especially when they were in action!

*Credit: Photographer, August Thieme, Jr.; Curt Tillotson Collection.*

No. 4568 (Ms-class 2-8-2): drivers, 63"; engine weight, 272,900 lbs.; steam pressure, 200 lbs.; tractive effort, 53,900 lbs.; superheated; Baldwin built, 1913; tender weight (loaded with 8,000 gal. of water and 12 tons of coal); 153,000 lbs.; engine & tender length, 77' 7/8"; engine height, 15'1"; built-up trailer trucks; retired, May of 1950.

Passing through Union, S. C. is an extra northbound freight powered by one of the Southern's most handsome Ms-class 2-8-2's, No. 4568, shown pulling 66 cars this Aug. 1, 1948, with highway U. S. 176 seen to the right.

Since there was a slight grade north of town and those heavy 66 cars tied to the rear of No. 4568's tender, the engineer had to work his throttle and sanders just right in order for the "shotgunning" 2-8-2 to maintain traction with the rails as this long freight from Columbia, S.C.'s Andrews Yard is shown heading to Spartanburg, S. C.'s Haynes Yard.

There were no doubts that the citizens of Union knew that a hard-working Southern freight was passing through town as a result of the sounds coming from No. 4569 which was using every ounce of its 53,900 lbs. of tractive effort to keep its train moving. Within 28 miles, the heavy freight would enter the Washington-Atlanta main line in north Spartanburg, work upgrade by the city's passenger station and enter the long Haynes Yard.

Ms-class 2-8-2's were used system-wide, except for the lines with weight restrictions such as that part of the Southern's Meridian, Miss. And New Orleans, La. segment of its Washington-New Orleans route, as well as the road's route from Danville, Ky. to St. Louis, Mo. line. The heavier and more efficient Ms-4, 2-8-2's became the standard main line freight power. As a result, the lighter 2-8-2's were used in other areas of the Southern. Most all the M-class Mikados were still in service until the number of diesels arriving on the road grew in such quantity that by June 17, 1953, the Southern became one of the first major roads to be 100% dieselized.

Like all the other steam power on the Southern, the M-class "Mikes" received that extra care (called the "Southern touch") and were among the most esthetically pleasing 2-8-2's on any railroad.

*Credit: August Thieme, Jr.; Curt Tillotson Collection.*

No. 6267 (Ms-class 2-8-2): drivers, 63"; engine weight, 272,900 lbs.; steam pressure, 200 lbs.; tractive effort, 53,900 lbs.; superheated; Baldwin built, 1911; tender weight (loaded with 8,000 gal. of water and 12 tons of coal); 153,000 lbs.; engine & tender length, 77' 7/8"; engine height, 15'1"; built-up trailer trucks; retired, Dec. of 1949.

This photo clearly explains why a railroad's main line attracts so many railfans. You never know what to expect. Sure, there were regularly scheduled trains. However, what type of motive power would they have? And, if an extra movement approached, what would it be? Branch, even secondary lines, are usually predictable as to what trains you would see and what type of power would be used.

Here is a prime example of why a main line was (and remains) so popular among those who enjoy watching and/or photographing tonnage on the move. This exposure was made at Atlanta's Inman Yard as Southern's No. 53 (nicknamed the "Kieser Special") departs with the usual Ms-class 2-8-2 up front. Then that main line "mystique" happened. Behind that super clean, white colored driver rims, walkways and graphite-covered smoke box of No. 6267 was an even more beautiful, green and gold colored, "shining in the sun," Ts-class 4-8-2, No. 1453!!!

Talk about being lucky: the photographer not only found a double-headed freight passing in front of his camera's lens; he captured both freight and passenger engines, making up the power for the double-header on film; and, as a result, we all profit from his good fortune-that's for sure!

During the steam era when an engine received major shopping, it would be assigned to a local freight or a regular freight that did a great deal of stopping, starting and switching, so all the new parts on the shopped engine would have a chance to fit into place. After a few such runs, the engine would be inspected by the shop crews; if everything appeared in good condition and the engineers who operated the engine could not find anything wrong, the engine would be returned to its normal duties. In this particular case, the elegant 4-8-2, No. 1453, would resume its job of pulling passenger trains for the Southern in mountainous territory.

So this Sept. 10, 1947 (3:30 p.m.) event would always remain a spectacular drama, which, unlike hundreds of other similar happenings, was captured on film for generations of railfans to come, who could see and marvel at such an event.

Just look at No. 6267-as clean as possible-sanding heavily in order to get the tonnage moving and the beautiful "lady" behind the hard-working Ms-class 2-8-2, glistening in her new paint job-a Ts-class Mountain-all working together, making Southern officials happy and the railfans ecstatic! Yes, the main line was the place to be if you wanted to wait for the unexpected and-if you were lucky-catch the action on film.

The reaction to this spectacular view for me would be: AWESOME!

*Credit: Photographer, Unknown; Curt Tillotson Collection.*

No. 6601 (Ms-class 2-8-2): drivers, 63"; engine weight, 272,900 lbs.; steam pressure, 200 lbs.; tractive effort, 53,900 lbs.; superheated; Baldwin built, 1913; tender weight (loaded with 8,000 gal. of water and 12 tons of coal); 153,000 lbs.; engine & tender length, 77' 7/8"; engine height, 15'1"; built-up trailer trucks; retired, Oct. of 1951.

Even though it only had 63" drivers and 53,900 lbs. of tractive effort, Southern's Ms-class 2-8-2's could make good time "IF" the tonnage was not too great, there were "big rails" to operate on and the area did not have too many grades.

This Southern "Mike," No. 6601 (formerly assigned to the AGS-Alabama Great Southern-segment of the system) proved its ability to pull a freight in the 55+ m.p.h. range as shown here on the Atlanta-Birmingham main line, passing through Chattahoochee, Ga. with a westbound extra freight in mid-afternoon on June 12, 1946, with that beautiful sounding steamboat whistle tied down for the few crossings in the area.

Speaking of beautiful things, look at this fast-moving Ms-class 2-8-2: graphite on its smoke box and stack, the engine jacket and tender sides were quite clean and the overall appearance looked so right or, as a model railroader would say-everything about No. 6601 was "to scale."

The Mikados-especially the elegant and effective Ms-4's (the standard main line freight power for the Southern until the arrival of the diesels)-were the favorite freight engines on the road. Like the 2-8-0 Consolidations, which the 2-8-2's replaced, the "Mikes" proved to be most versatile and could be used in practically any service and go anywhere on the Southern except where weight restrictions would not permit the 2-8-2's to roam.

Look at that old, wood-sided Seaboard Air Line "watermelon" car tucked in behind No. 6601's tender. For sure, the end of its service days was near.

Action: that's what we see here speeding down the high iron during a time when being a railfan was somewhat more enjoyable and less "stressful."

*Credit: Photographer, Unknown; Curt Tillotson Collection.*

No. 4768 (Ms-1 class 2-8-2):drivers, 63"; engine weight, 292,000 lbs.; steam pressure, 200 lbs.; superheated; tractive effort, 54,600 lbs.; Richmond built, 1923; tender weight (loaded with 10,000 gal. of water and 16 tons of coal); 185,400 lbs.; engine & tender length, 81'11"; engine height, 14'11"; Hodges trailer trucks; retired, Nov. of 1952 (sold to the Baltimore Steel Co.).

Look at the edge of the ballast on the double track roadbed: deep with black cinders. This could only be caused by a great number of steam-powered trains that passed through this area.

One of those "cinder makers" is shown heading west with 32 cars of an extra freight near Austell, Ga. late in the afternoon on Dec. 14, 1946, heading towards Birmingham from Atlanta-at a good rate of speed or, as the old saying goes, it was "balling the jack."

No. 4768, a Southern Ms-1 class 2-8-2, could make good time with short freights. Those white flags were standing straight back; the engineer had his sanders on since there was a slight grade in the area and he wanted those 63" drivers to keep traction with the "big rails" so he could arrive in Birmingham on time. The fireman was shown enjoying the view as he had the stoker on in order to keep his steam pressure up to the "company notch," i.e., 200 lbs. That nearly clear stack was deceptive, for cinders were shooting out, eventually adding to the depth of those already on the right-of-way.

This exposure is a perfect example of how it was when steam ruled the rails: you would hear a steamboat whistle off in the distance; then you saw a smug of smoke on the horizon. A "machine gun"-like exhausting black steam locomotive approached you and the ground began to tremble as flailing rods were "clanking" with great rapidity as the "iron horse" passed by with a long string of cars trailing behind its tender. As the freight disappeared, you heard that melodious whistle becoming softer and softer. That's the way it was in the steam era. Even though the train was gone, your heart was still beating at a rapid pace and your mind was still absorbing all that you had just witnessed. It was GREAT!

*Credit: Photographer, Unknown; Curt Tillotson Collection.*

No. 6291 (Ms-1 class 2-8-2): drivers, 63"; engine weight, 292,000 lbs.; steam pressure, 200 lbs.; tractive effort, 54,600 lbs.; superheated; Schenectady built, 1918; tender weight (loaded with 10,000 gal. of water and 16 tons of coal); 185,400 lbs.; Hodges trailer trucks; engine & tender length, 81'11"; engine height, 14'11"; retired, Nov. of 1952 (sold to the Baltimore Steel Co.). The color of the tracks tells the story of this area.

When a Southern freight departed their yard in Cincinnati, it would cross over the huge, impressive double-track bridge over the Ohio River. On the south side of the bridge the Southern's CNO&TP (Cincinnati, New Orleans and Texas Pacific) passed through Ludlow, Ky. and immediately faced one of the most difficult grades on this main line to Chattanooga: Earlanger Hill.

On this grade, most all southbound freights required a "pusher" engine, even passenger trains with more cars than usual also needed help to overcome this stiff climb.

Just look at the southbound rails as compared to the northbound main line. The tremendous sanding required to keep traction with the rails was grounded into them over 30 times each day, day after day, year after year until they were white while the northbound tracks remained its normal color. Even today's diesel "monsters" have to do quite a large amount of sanding so they can use their massive horsepower in order to master the hill.

It's early morning in Oct. of 1943, when the photographer heard the "shotgunning" exhaust of a steam-powered freight train approaching his location.

Within minutes, he sees a Southern Ms-1 class 2-8-2, No. 6291, with a larger than usual smoke stack, an engine as clean as possible with the graphite-covered smoke box and stack and white flags still white-these flags indicated that this was a southbound extra freight.

Without a "helper" No. 6291-assigned to the CNO&TP-was down to approximately 15 m.p.h. but still moving. The sand in this area was so deep that it actually covered the tops of the crossties!

A steam-powered freight working upgrade with a great deal of tonnage tied to its tail, would produce a drama that simply could not be reproduced by any other form of motive power. It was a thrilling event. The sight, sounds and the smell of smoke, hot steam and grease just enhanced the moment. The driver rods, making a complete revolution after four engine exhausts, were "clanking" so loud that it made you think they would "fly off" at any minute. It was simply a sight that captivated you and reinforced your love of trains, especially those powered by a big, black fire-breathing steam locomotive, down "on its knees" but keeping its tonnage moving to its destination.

It was a time now long gone but never forgotten!

*Credit: Photographer, Collection of C. K. Marsh; Curt Tillotson Collection.*

# Ms-4 Class Heavy Mikados: 2-8-2's

During the early part of the 20th Century, the Southern's fleet of 2-8-0 Consolations were among the most effective motive power on their roster. Indeed, the Southern had such admiration and faith in their 2-8-0's performance, they eventually possessed one of the largest fleet of Consolations among all railroads in our country.

As the likelihood of a world war approached, things began to change in the rail world (this included the Southern as well). The demands for stronger motive power increased along with longer trains; the rolling stock grew larger and heavier plus the need for increased speed became essential. These new parameters facing the Southern and other roads were simply too great for the Consolations to fulfill, even with their newest and most powerful 2-8-0's. As a result, the Southern became interested in a new wheel arrangement. The 2-8-2 type engines, with its larger firebox, greater steaming capacity and its ability to pull more tonnage faster, caused the road to purchase their first batch of 2-8-2's from Baldwin in 1911 and they were numbered in the 4500 to 4600 series; they were classified as "Ms" locomotives.

As a point of interest, the Southern's first 2-8-2, No. 4501, would become the most popular and famous of all the hundreds of Mikados owned by the Southern AFTER the road had become fully dieselized in 1953. In the late 1960's, this first 2-8-2 was painted green and gold, received white colored rims for its driver and pony trucks; it played a major role in creating the most wonderful and sorely missed "steam excursion era," which lasted into the early 1990's. Of all the engines used during those glorious days for railfans, No. 4501 was, arguably, the most esthetically pleasing in appearance and performance. The beautifully colored "little giant" passed through my home of Oxford, N. C. on four occasions, followed by five visits of 2-8-0 No. 722. To this day, No. 4501 makes an occasional run in and around its home base of Chattanooga, TN.

Throughout the years, the demands on the Southern increased. As a result, the road acquired more and more 2-8-2's: Ms-1's, Ms-2's, all the way through the Ms-7 series. However, the class of "Mikes" that proved so effective that they became the Southern's major and standard main line motive power and remained so until the diesels won the war of rail power. The class that emerged as the major locomotive was the Ms-4's. They were numbered 4800 through No. 4914 for the road; No. 6320 through No. 6337 for the Southern's CNO&TP; No. 6622 through No. 6629 for the AGS and more.

The Ms-4's controlled the major freight assignments on the Washington-Atlanta main line, Atlanta to Chattanooga and Macon. You could also find them on the run from Greensboro to Selma, N. C. and, over the ACL, through trackage rights, to Pinners Point, Va.; eventually, they were used between Charlotte to Columbia, S. C. and even in and around the Birmingham area.

The first group of Ms-4's (No. 4800 through No. 4845) had the big Worthington feedwater heater while the remainder were equipped with the most effective and handsome Elesco feedwater heater. Indeed, to many railfans, those Ms-4's which had the Elesco heater placed in front of their smokestacks, were second only to the magnificent Ps-4 heavy Pacifics in both beauty and pleasing symmetry (I am one of those who felt-and still feel-this to be a true statement). An Elesco fitted Ms-4 2-8-2, really making good time with a long line of tonnage hooked onto its tender, traveling up and down the main line with that steamboat whistle tied down by the engineer, was a sight to behold-one that when seen was not soon forgotten!

During World War II, motive power became so scarce on the Southern that they purchased seven second-hand Erie 2-8-2's. They were classed as Ms-7's and became the only 2-8-2's on the road with Vanderbilt tenders. After WWII, they were removed from the Southern's roster. And, in the late 1920's, the road found themselves with a surplus of 2-10-2's; and the Southern began a program to remove one set of drivers and made them among the most powerful "Mikes" on the road which classified them as Ms-5 and Ms-6's. However, only 5 were converted to 2-8-2's since the Great Depression occurred, making it economically impossible to continue the program due to lack of funds.

Even with all these changes in their 2-8-2's, the Southern's Ms-4's were the "king of the road" until replaced by the products of mostly General Motor's Electro-Motive Division (EMD)'s diesel-electrics.

They were truly elegant engines that performed with great effectiveness for the Southern for many years. It is most regretful that at least one of the Ms-4's was not preserved, like Southern's famous Ps-4 class heavy Pacific No. 1401, so future generations could see what a steam powered freight engine looked like during the period from 1923 to 1953 — 30 years of getting the tonnage and, when needed, passengers to their destinations.

No. 4914 (Ms-4 class heavy 2-8-2): drivers, 63"; engine weight, 326,000 lbs.; steam pressure, 200 lbs.; tractive effort, 59,600 lbs.; superheated; Baldwin built, 1928; tender weight (loaded with 10,000 gal. of water and 16 tons of coal); 191,400 lbs.; engine & tender length, 83' 1/16"; engine height, 14'11"; Elesco feedwater heater; standard stoker; Hodges trailer trucks; retired, Nov. of 1952.

This photo gives you an idea of why a railroad's main line was the place to be if you were a railfan in the days of steam operations (and it remains so, even with diesels pulling the tonnage), for a branch line had certain trains and motive power you could count on. A main line, however, had not only regular scheduled trains, but, on occasion, something special would pass by and/or you might find unusual motive power keeping the rails shiny.

The Southern's Washington-Atlanta main line was one of these magical places to be (and remains so even under the Norfolk Southern control). Not only was this particular extra movement — shown here, special — it was a run the Southern officials wish they had more of since it was a money-making "peach special," pulled by the road's top of the line motive power and making a good 40-45 m.p.h. and climbing!

This was Extra 4914 North passing through the "Furniture Capital of the World," High Point, N. C., this early afternoon on Aug. 13, 1947. The extra was powered by a beautiful Ms-4 heavy Mikado with a solid refrigerator ("reefer") train which originated from Spartanburg, S. C. At their Haynes Yard, the "reefers" were all iced and made ready for a quick run north towards Alexandria, Va.'s Potomac Yard where motive power would be changed in order to carry the extra's cargo on to New York City. The delicious South Carolina peaches would be consumed quickly by the happy New Yorkers.

With Alexandria 299 miles away, the "reefers" would not have to be re-iced until the extra north arrived at "Pot Yard."

During the peach season, local freights would bring in cars loaded with the delicious fruit to Spartanburg. Here they would be iced and assembled into a solid train. Then, main line motive power took the train north "ASAP." These trains were priority movements and traveled at near passenger train speed.

Look at the beautiful white trim on the Southern's Elesco feedwater heater equipped, heavy 2-8-2; No. 4914's engine jacket and tender were spotless and shiny clean. The Southern's reputation of giving their locomotives a great deal of care was clearly demonstrated in this exciting photo. By the way, the bridge in the background-above the double track main line-was actually a pedestrian walkway. Over the years, I made several excellent photos from this same walkway. Alas, it was dismantled a few years ago. However, the position where the photographer made this outstanding exposure remains there to this day. It is still a great place for rail photographers to make exposures of the great number of freight trains of the Norfolk Southern passing by. There are also six Amtrak passenger trains passing through High Point on a daily basis: No. 73 and No. 74, the "Piedmont," No. 79 and No. 80, the "Carolinian" and No. 19 and No. 20, the "Crescent." Both the "Carolinian" and the "Piedmont" are daylight runs.

High Point remains a great place to be in order to see and photograph the ebb and flow of a busy, modern, "hot" main line in action.

*Credit: Photographer, August Thieme, Jr.; Curt Tillotson Collection.*

No. 4875 (Ms-4 class heavy 2-8-2): drivers, 63"; engine weight, 326,000 lbs.; steam pressure, 200 lbs.; tractive effort, 59,600 lbs.; superheated; Richmond (Alco) built, 1926; tender weight (loaded with 10,000 gal. of water and 16 tons of coal); 191,400 lbs.; engine & tender length, 83' 1/6"; engine height, 14'11"; Elesco feedwater heater; Standard stocker; Hodges trailer trucks; retired, Aug. of 1953 (sold to the Baltimore Steel Co.).

I ask you: have you ever seen a more handsome heavy Mikado at the head of a long, priority freight in action? Graphited smoke box, white trim on the driver and pony trucks, walkways and the bottom of the cowcatcher, shiny clean engine jacket and tender plus gold colored numbers and lettering: these items simply helped to enhance the esthetically pleasing appearance of a Southern Ms-4 class 2-8-2. No. 4875 is shown nearing Reidsville, N. C. on the Danville Division portion of the busy Washington-Atlanta main line this beautiful morning in August of 1948.

Shown here is Southern's "hot shot" No. 153, at approximately 9:35 a.m. at a good 40-45 m.p.h. with its engineer trying to gain as much speed as possible since there was a slight grade plus an "S" curve leading into the town where tobacco products dominated its economy, so that No. 153 would maintain its fast schedule on its way to Atlanta and points south.

These tobacco products (cigarettes, cigars, etc.) brought in a good deal of revenue for the Southern. In fact, at the time of this photo, the Southern had a big, powerful 0-8-0 switcher stationed in Reidsville to help serve the tobacco companies and other businesses located there.

Reidsville was so important to the Southern that several of their passenger trains made stops there. I used to be amazed at just how many main line varnishes were listed on the passenger station's schedule board. And, up until a few years ago, the station was a favorite location for me to photograph the many trains passing through town, even when it was raining, for it shed protected both me and my camera from the elements while making exposures of a hot main line in action. Now the station is gone and only Amtrak's "Crescent" passes through at speed in both directions during the night. Freight traffic is still brisk on the now Norfolk Southern main line but, unfortunately, the vast majority of traffic flows through town during the night hours. I have a saying that describes this dilemma: "When the sun goes down, the trains come out; when the sun comes up, however, most of the trains disappear!"

During those days when the beautiful Ms-4's headed the freights and the elegant, green and gold colored Ps-4's handled the passenger traffic, trains rumbled through Reidsville constantly both day and night. Indeed, by 1948, it was not unusual to have 50-75 or more trains in a 24-hour period, to pass through town on this historic, double track main line.

It was great being a railfan in the "good old days!"

*Credit: Photographer, David Driscoll; Curt Tillotson Collection.*

No. 4884 (Ms-4 class heavy 2-8-2): drivers, 63"; engine weight, 326,000 lbs.; steam pressure, 200 lbs.; tractive effort, 59,600 lbs.; superheated; Richmond built, 1926; tender weight (loaded with 10,000 gal. of water and 16 tons of coal); 191,400 lbs.; engine & tender length, 83' 1/16"; engine height 14'11"; Elesco feedwater heater; Standard stoker; Hodges trailer trucks; retired, Nov. of 1952 (sold to the Baltimore Steel Co.).

Here is a sight railroaders would prefer not to see since it meant there was trouble up the line; however, some railfans would find this special movement intriguing.

There was a derailment at Lynchburg, Va.'s Montview Yard. Quickly, the "big hook" was sent south out of Monroe, Va. to try and get things back to normal conditions. However, when the Monroe extra arrived at the scene, they knew they would need help. The Southern sent the "big hook" from Spencer, N. C. to assist in the cleanup.

Shown here is Extra 4884 North hurrying to the derailment to work on the "mess" from the south end while the boys from Monroe worked from the north side.

Southern's Ms-4 heavy Mikado, No. 4884, was assigned to the "Derrick train," a.k.a. the "Big Hook." Even though it was a work extra, look how clean, white wheeled and handsome No. 4884 appeared this cloudy afternoon in April of 1951, moving at the 30 m.p.h. pace permitted when pulling a "Derrick train," as it approached Altavista, Va.-approximately 27 miles south of Lynchburg.

The bridge at Altavista was and remains a hot spot for railfans since it was high, long and photogenic with a great deal of rail traffic. The bridge not only enabled the Washington-Atlanta main line to span the Staunton River but it also crossed over the main line of the Virginian Railroad at the north end of the magnificent structure. In 1959, the N&W purchased the Virginian in order to get their coal trains to Norfolk, Va. without facing that grueling grade up to Blue Ridge, Va. Then, in 1982, the current Norfolk Southern was created and the NS uses the old Virginian as if it was their eastbound main line while their westbound main passed through Lynchburg.

There is no doubt in my mind that, next to the green and gold colored Ps-4 heavy Pacifics (especially those with Elesco feedwater heater and six axle tenders), the Southern Ms-4 heavy 2-8-2's (with the attractive Elesco heater) were among my favorite engines during the days of steam operations. Most railfans would agree with my opinion concerning the Ms-4's, which dominated the freight power on the main line for over two decades. Boy, you could clearly see that No. 4884's fireman had opened his stoker and the engineer had his throttle way back on is quadrant, as this 2-8-2 headed towards the "City of Seven Hills"-Lynchburg.

Look at the extra's consist: the "Big Hook," a tank of water, extra track panels, a coach for the work crew to sleep in if they could not complete their work in one day, plus the caboose for No. 4884's crew. This was a side of railroading rarely seen by the public. Notice the smoke stains on the Southern's bridge left there by the Virginian's 2-8-4's, 2-6-6-6's and other steam power!

*Credit: Photographer, Collection of Shelby Lowe; Curt Tillotson Collection.*

No. 4863 (Ms-4 class heavy 2-8-2): drivers, 63"; engine weight, 326,000 lbs.; steam pressure, 200 lbs.; tractive effort, 59,600 lbs.; superheated; Schenectady built, 1924; tender weight (loaded with 10,000 gal. of water and 16 tons of coal); 191,400 lbs.; engine & tender length, 83' 1/16"; engine height, 14'11"; Elesco feedwater heater; Standard stoker; Hodges trailer truck; retired, Nov. of 1952 (sold to the Baltimore Steel Co.).

After picking up a few "hot" cars (four loads of cigarettes), Southern's 1st No. 57 is shown departing Reidsville, N. C. with a vengeance! The engineer of 1st No. 57 had his throttle wide open, sanders on and his engine bell ringing as the long freight heads south on the Danville Division portion of the Washington-Atlanta main line with Greensboro, N. C. (approximately 25 miles away) being its next stop. Quite often when a freight runs in several sections, the first train will do a great deal of setting off and picking up cars at key points along the main line.

With several tobacco plants in town, making cigarettes, cigars and other tobacco products-high revenue business-Reidsville was one of those "key points."

The long freight was fighting a short grade as you can tell by looking at the trailing cars "drop off" in the background. Once the engineer gets about half of his train over this "hump," the Ms-4 heavy 2-8-2, No. 4863, would really roll since it was mostly down-grade all the way to the "Gate City"-Greensboro-where 1st No. 57 would work Pomona Yard.

With that loud "shotgunning" of No. 4863, the people nearby stopped whatever they were doing to witness this soul-stirring drama on this beautiful morning in Sept. of 1948. Within 5 years, such steam action will disappear, replaced by the "growling" of diesels. Notice that both tracks in the area are white in appearance. Trains entering Reidsville from either the north or south had a grade to face. As a result, the citizens of this attractive town could hear trains approaching several minutes before roaring by the town's passenger station (to the right of 1st No. 57, in the background). This would be my kind of location to get excellent exposures of the great number of north and southbound rail movements since you had time to select your "spot" to make your "shots" because of those grades. Today's Norfolk Southern still provides a great deal of rail action in the Reidsville area. Unfortunately, the majority of trains pass through town during the night hours. However, it is a main line and, as such, you can expect anything at anytime-day or night. But the diesels cannot produce the unforgettable action produced by the steam-powered trains, especially those pulled by the impressive Ms-4 heavy Mikados with an impatient engineer (notice that huge steamboat whistle on top of No. 4863). Now, look out for the falling cinders!

*Credit: Photographer, David Driscoll; Curt Tillotson Collection.*

No. 4856 (Ms-4 class heavy 2-8-2): drivers, 63"; engine weigh, 326,000 lbs.; steam pressure, 200 lbs.; tractive effort, 59,600 lbs.; superheated; Schenectady built, 1924; tender weight (loaded with 10,000 gal. of water and 16 tons of coal); 191,400 lbs.; engine & tender length, 83' 1/16"; engine height, 14'11"; Elesco feedwater heater; Standard stoker; Hodges trailer trucks; retired, Nov. of 1952 (sold to the Baltimore Steel Co.).

Here is one of the locations where my love of trains was nurtured over the years and my desire to photograph the action of main line railroading was encouraged: Danville, Va.

Southern's No. 57 had picked up and set off cars at Danville's Dundee Yard-less than a mile north of this location and across the double track Dan River bridge-and was now passing through the historic passenger station with a handsome and powerful Ms-4 class 2-8-2, No. 4856-an engine as clean as possible with graphite covering its smoke box, white trimmed wheels and shiny engine jacket and tender.

Notice the engineer was looking down at the ground. He was gauging his gathering speed as he made sure that the heavy 2-8-2 did not lose traction as the big "MIKE" prepared to do battle with the major obstacle all southbound trains had to face when leaving Danville (and today's SD-70's, CW40-9D's and other similar diesel "monsters" of motive power still have to overcome this challenge): Cemetery Hill!

It might not look it, but No. 4856 was working as hard as its 59,600 lbs. of tractive effort would permit. The fireman was a "company man," since he had the big "MIKE," heading south, with a clear stack (a clear stack meant he was not wasting coal and was saving the "company" money). Cemetery Hill was a sharp grade-approximately two miles long-which meant a great challenge to those freights which had to work Dundee. Southern trains that did not stop at Dundee could have enough momentum to overcome the "hill;" however, like No. 57, there was not a great amount of level track for a southbound train to gain enough momentum for the climb. As a result, this heavy "MIKE" would have to go up and over the obstacle with sheer power. Even during the diesel era, I have seen freights stall on the grade and one of the Dundee switchers would have to couple to its rear and help push the train up the grade. During the steam era, a powerful 0-8-0 from Dundee would have to help southbound freights to overcome gravity. Fortunately, No. 57's tonnage was just enough to enable No. 4856 to get its train over Cemetery Hill this day.

At the time of this exposure, the traffic through the passenger station was great. Not only did the Southern's fleet of passenger trains stop there; by August 14, 1947, the passenger trains to and from Richmond, Va. originated and/or terminated at the station as well.

Danville was the place to be to witness the parade of both freight and passenger runs-day and night-pulled by the green and gold colored Ps-4's as well as the light Ps-2's and the attractive Ms-4 heavy "MIKES."

Yes, my desire to be a railfan was increased each and every time I took a trip to Danville and the surrounding area-it was (and remains) great!

*Photographer, August A. Thieme, Jr.; Curt Tillotson Collection.*

No. 4913 (Ms-4 class heavy 2-8-2): drivers, 63"; engine weight, 326,000 lbs.; steam pressure, 200 lbs.; tractive effort, 59,600 lbs.; superheated; Baldwin built, 1928; tender weight (loaded with 10,000 gal. of water and 16 tons of coal); 191,400 lbs.; engine & tender length, 83' 1/16"; engine height, 14'11"; Elesco feedwater heater; Standard stoker; Hodges trailer trucks; retired, Oct. 17, 1952 (sold to the Baltimore Steel Co.).

Lynchburg, Va., known as the "City of Seven Hills," is another great location for railfans to view a parade of trains provided by the Norfolk Southern and CSX. During the days of steam operations, the number of trains passing through this beautiful city was almost unbelievable. Three main lines provided these wonderful encounters: the Southern, Norfolk & Western and the C&O's James River line.

There was another reason for Lynchburg's attraction for those who love to watch and/or photograph rail action. It was a place to witness the passage of some of the most attractive and powerful steam powered trains in our country. Leading the "attractive" aspect of this great location was the Southern Railway with their renowned and regal, green and gold colored Ps-4 heavy Pacifics and their equally handsome class Ms-4 type of heavy 2-8-2's, which was the standard freight power for all Washington-Atlanta freight movements (and would remain so until the arrival of the diesel-electric locomotives).

Along with a vast number of beautiful trains, there was a third factor which caused Lynchburg to become (and remain) one of the most favorite places to be for main line action was the fact that, being the "City of Seven Hills," there were numerous bridges: long bridges, high bridges, extremely attractive and photogenic bridges. The Southern's James River Bridge-located approximately 4-5 miles from the city-is still one of the "seven wonders of the rail world," in my opinion. And just north of the famous and historic Southern's Kemper Street Station, there is another bridge that spans a deep ravine plus the N&W's passenger main line.

On this curved bridge, heading south just out of Monroe, Va. (7.4 miles to the north) is a magnificent Southern Ms-4 Mikado pulling No. 51 towards Spencer, N. C. and points south on the Washington-Atlanta main line this early morning on a warm August 15, 1947.

The engineer of No. 4913 had just closed his throttle (notice the smoke off to the right) as he prepared to pass through Kemper St. Station on its way to the city's Montview Yard. The "boys" at Monroe had really prepared No. 4913 for this assignment. Just look at the white trim on its running boards, the bottom of its cowcatcher, the pony trucks and driver rims; the engine jacket and tender where shiny clean and the heavy "Mike" was in good operational condition as well.

This, believe it or not, was a common sight in the Lynchburg area at the time of this photo-a sight just "begging" to be photographed. What are all those barrels (on the right) doing there? Even though the vast majority of the bridge was built with steel, there were areas of wood (the crossties being just one example) on the bridge as well. If a fire developed, it could be extinguished by the water in those barrels plus, if you got caught walking on the bridge as a train was approaching, the area holding those barrels offered you a place of safety to occupy until the train passed by.

This was my kind of railroad, my kind of location, my kind of locomotive, my kind of train, my kind of way to start a day for photographing steam powered trains in the Lynchburg area, especially those elegant Southern Railway "iron horses."

*Credit: Photographer, August A. Thieme, Jr.; Curt Tillotson Collection.*

No.4903 (Ms-4 class heavy 2-8-2): drivers, 63"; engine weight, 326,000 lbs.; steam pressure, 200 lbs.; tractive effort, 59,600 lbs.; superheated; Baldwin built, 1928; tender weight (loaded with 10,000 gal. of water and 16 tons of coal); 191,400 lbs.; engine & tender length, 83' 1/16"; engine height, 14'11"; Elesco feedwater heater; Standard stoker; Hodges trailer trucks; retired, Oct. of 1952 (sold to the Baltimore Steel Co.).

Early during this morning in Nov. of 1948, a big Southern Ms-4 class 2-8-2, No. 4903, pulled out of Monroe, Va. wearing white flags-indicating it was an extra movement. When the handsome "Mike" departed this railroad town, which was the beginning of the Danville Division portion of the Washington-Atlanta main line, No. 4903 headed south with only a caboose tied to its clean tender (this is called a "caboose hop"). Why did this powerful, standard main line freight engine just have a caboose without any freight cars in its consist?

The Virginian Railroad had left a long line of loaded coal cars for the Southern at Altavista, Va.-30.1 miles south of Monroe. After a quick trip over the James River Bridge, the Extra 4903 South passed through Lynchburg, Va.'s Kemper Street passenger station and the city's Montview Yard, finally arriving at Altavista. Then the extra backed down the connection track, picked up the cut of coal loaded with hopper cars, placed its "crummy" on the rear of the train, returned to the double track main line and then made preparations to head for Spencer, N. C.'s historic yard-named after the first President of the Southern Railway, Samuel Spencer (1894-1906).

Extra 4903 South is shown just out of Altavista, approaching the little community of Motley, Va. And that deep, melodious steamboat whistle was sounding a warning for an approaching crossing, hoping that no one would dare try beating the large Ms-4 to the crossing.

The 4903, even on a coal drag, had the white trim on its running boards, cowcatcher and driver rims. And the 2-8-2 was working hard to build up as much speed and momentum as possible since a long grade into Gretna, Va. was nearby. And with the heavy loaded coal cars it was carrying, No. 4903, even with its impressive 59,600 lbs. of tractive effort, will need all of its power, its speed and momentum to get its train over the grade and on to Spencer.

This was my kind of railroading: main line action provided by a big, beautiful Ms-4 class steam engine.

*Credit: Photographer, H. Stafford Bryant, Jr.; Curt Tillotson Collection.*

No. 4862 (Ms-4 class heavy 2-8-2): drivers, 63"; engine weight, 326,000 lbs.; steam pressure, 200 lbs.; tractive effort, 59,600 lbs.; superheated; Schenectady built, 1924; tender weight (loaded with 10,000 gal. of water and 16 tons of coal); 191,400 lbs.; engine & tender length, 83' 1/16"; engine height, 14'11"; Elesco feedwater heater; Standard stoker; Hodges trailer trucks; retired, Nov. of 1952.

In a previous photo, we witnessed a big, beautiful Southern Ms-4 class 2-8-2 passing through the Danville, Va.'s passenger station, after crossing over the Dan River Bridge, fighting to gain as much momentum as possible, for it and all southbound trains had to face the formidable grade known as "Cemetery Hill."

In this exposure, we were on the north side of the Dan River Bridge and we had another handsome Southern Ms-4 heavy Mikado, No. 4862, making time as it headed north with No. 56, this early morning on May 20, 1940, passing through Dundee, Va. and the yard for the Danville area.

The big "girl" had built up a great deal of speed after descending Cemetery Hill; now the 2-8-2 tried to gain additional momentum (notice the sanders were on) as it prepared to face a grade that was longer than the Cemetery Hill, one that was far more famous. For ahead of No. 56 and the train was a long confrontation with White Oak Mountain. This was an area that gained notoriety in the song about the "Wreck of Old 97," since this was the mountain where engineer "Steve Broady" lost his brakes "on Sept. 27, 1903," and jumped off the trestle near Danville and became part of the lexicon in rail history.

No. 56's bell was ringing since it was approaching a narrow highway crossing which was next to Dundee Tower (to the right and out of the exposure-just behind the photographer). Even though No. 4862 was 96 miles north of Spencer, N. C. where it took control of No. 56, which originated in Atlanta, the work of the "boys" at Spencer was still obvious: look at the clean graphite on the 2-8-2's smoke box, silver cylinder heads, white trimmed driver wheels and walkways. And the engine jacket and tender sides sparkled in the early morning sun.

No. 4910 (Ms-4 class heavy 2-8-2): drivers, 63"; engine weight, 326,000 lbs; steam pressure, 200 lbs.; tractive effort, 59,600 lbs.; superheated; Baldwin built, 1928; tender weight (loaded with 10,000 gal. of water and 16 tons of coal); 191,400 lbs.; engine & tender length, 83' 1/16"; engine height, 14'11"; Elesco feedwater heater; Standard stoker; Hodges trailer trucks; retired, Nov. of 1952.

Here is where I spend many railfan trips over the years in order to photograph rail action on the Southern's historic and busy Washington-Atlanta main line: the passenger station at Reidsville, N.C. The station's shed helped me to be able to cover the ebb and flow of trains (even when it was raining). And it also gave me some relief from the oppressive heat from the sun during the summertime.

When I started recording main line rail scenes in Reidsville, the beautiful "bulldog-nosed" F-3's and my favorite, the F-7's, dominated the freight power-along with the E-7's and "the most attractive diesel ever made" (in my opinion), the E-8's-headed the passenger power. Over the years, I made numerous exposures of GM's: GP-30's, GP-35's, SD-24's, SD-35's, SD-40's, SD-45's, GP-38's, GP-49's, GP-50's, GP-60's, plus such GE "motors" as U-30C's, U-33C's, U-23B's, B23-7's, B30-7A1's, etc.

This photo, however, gives both you and I an idea of what it was like when Southern's attractive Ms-4 class heavy Mikados were the standard freight power on the main line for over two decade; the passenger runs were dominated by the colorful and elegant Ps-4 class heavy Pacifics-all passing through Reidsville many times each and every day and night. I believe that I would prefer covering rail action during the steam era as compared to my coverage of diesel power over the years!

On this morning in Sept. of 1944, you could hear a steamboat whistle blowing for several road crossings off to the north. You knew this meant a southbounder was on the way. From around the curve in the background, a big Elesco feedwater heater equipped Ms-4 heavy 2-8-2, No. 4910, came into view with freight No. 153, pulling up the slight grade, coming into Reidsville. Even though it was "shotgunning," the fireman had a nearly clear stack (that meant you would be showered with cinders). No. 4910 is shown passing by the busy passenger station (on the right) and freight depot (on the left) at near 25-30 m.p.h. Even during the war years, the Southern crews kept their engines looking beautiful and in good operational condition (look at that huge steamboat whistle next to the steam dome-WOW!).

This was a good example of how it was when the "iron horses" moved both tonnage and passengers during the war as well as peace times. Unfortunately, both stations are gone and now, however, the massive D9-40CW's, SD-70's and other huge diesels roll through town, providing the rail action today. Don't get me wrong, I enjoy observing these diesel leviathans that provide today's rail action, but the diesel action does not come even close to the magnificent scene provided by No. 4910 as it moved this Alexandria, Va.-Atlanta (and points south) freight, No. 153, towards its destination. Indeed, it was no contest. Steam scenes were unforgettable-just look at this photo!

*Credit: Photographer, David Driscoll; Curt Tillotson Collection.*

The Southern's reputation for giving extra care to each and every engine, treating them as if they were members of their family, was well deserved.

During the early 1940's, the volume of trains grew until it was not uncommon to have over 75 trains passing through the Danville-Dundee area each and every 24 hours, each and every day. And all the steam motive power were not only in good operational condition, they were all as clean and as attractive as any motive power on any railroad in our country. And this was just the freight power. As far as passenger power was concerned, all I need to say was that the vast number of Southern's fleet of varnish were powered by the colorful and renowned Ps-4's!

Boy, No. 4862 was really "picking 'em up and laying 'em down!"

*Credit: Photographer, Collection of C. W. Witbeck; Curt Tillotson Collection.*

No. 4809 (Ms-4 class heavy 2-8-2): drivers, 63"; engine weight, 326,000 lbs.; steam pressure, 200 lbs.; tractive effort, 59,600 lbs.; superheated; Richmond built, 1923; tender weight (loaded with 10,000 gal. of water and 16 tons of coal); 191,400 lbs.; engine & tender length, 83' 1/16"; engine height, 14'11"; Worthington feedwater heater; Standard stoker; Hodges trailer trucks; retired, April of 1952 (sold to the Baltimore Steel Co.).

After leaving Selma, N. C. and working the yard in Raleigh, N. C.-on its way to Greensboro, N. C. and the Washington-Atlanta main line-Southern's through freight No. 255 is shown leaving the state's capital city and heading west. Today's No. 255 was powered by a big Ms-4 class Mikado, No. 4809, with that huge Worthington feedwater heater hung just above the 2-8-2's No. 3 and No. 4 driver wheels, and was shown passing the most popular location in Raleigh for railfans (and it remains so to this very day with the Norfolk Southern, CSX and Amtrak providing the action): Boylan Tower (the tower was behind the Ms-4's tender in this photo).

At this location, the Southern's Goldsboro-Greensboro line was joined by the Seaboard Air Line's Richmond-Miami main line, forming a double track section that headed west 8.2 miles to Cary, N. C. (known as "Fetner" by rail employees). This was also the location where the old Norfolk Southern's Norfolk-Charlotte line crossed over the busy double track area. The number of trains passing through the Boylan area, especially during the steam era, was most impressive!

It was a warm afternoon in June of 1949, as No. 255's 71 cars headed out of the capital city, powered by No. 4809. Ahead of this lengthy freight was a long, steady grade to overcome, passing through Raleigh's beautiful Pullen Park, bisecting the campus of my alma mater-North Carolina State University-and on to Cary where No. 4809 would head its train west to Greensboro while the SAL turned south to Hamlet, N. C. and Miami.

The heavy "Mike" is shown starting up the long climb after passing under the Boylan St. bridge, crossing over the NS's main line with its sanders on. And the white capped fireman was relying on his Standard stoker to keep the big "girl" filled with enough steam in order to make it up the torturous grade.

The ground was trembling as the heavy and attractive "Mike" was really "digging in" with its white trimmed drivers, using the sand to keep traction with the rails. The sounds of No. 4809's exhaust was tremendous and yet exhilarating. This was an excellent example of steam at work, doing what it was designed to do, heading a long freight upgrade-unassisted-this glorious afternoon in '49. Man, this was railroading at its best!

*Credit: Photographer, Wiley Bryan; Curt Tillotson Collection.*

No. 4821 (Ms-4 class heavy 2-8-2): drivers, 63"; engine weight, 326,000 lbs.; steam pressure, 200 lbs.; tractive effort, 59,600 lbs.; superheated; Richmond built, 1923; tender weight (loaded with 10,000 gal. of water and 16 tons of coal); 191,400 lbs.; engine & tender length, 83' 1/16"; engine height, 14'11"; Worthington feed-water heater; Standard stoker; Hodges trailer trucks; retired, Aug. of 1953 (sold to the Baltimore Steel Co.).

The Danville-Dundee, Va. area-the two being separated by the Dan River-is located at the bottom of two grueling grades on the Southern's Washington-Atlanta main line. As a result, those trains that stopped there (passenger trains at Danville's historic station and freights at the yard in Dundee) had to try and build up as much momentum when departing the area. Those trains heading north had to prepare to take on the famous White Oak Mountain (where "Old 97" rode into rail history when it wrecked after descending the mountain too fast) while southbounders faced Cemetery Hill.

The grade over White Oak was longer and almost never required a "pusher" engine to help the train overcome the climb. However, Cemetery Hill was shorter and sharper in its rise. Several steam powered freights had to have one of the Dundee yard engines to couple on its rear to aid its battle over the hill. Indeed, I have witnessed diesel-powered freights leaving Dundee stalling on the grade. And, just as in the past, a switcher (this time a diesel engine) from Dundee would enter the main line and, with the road engines pulling and the switcher pushing, the freight would finally overcome this obstacle-an event almost as exciting as when it was performed by steam power!

Shown here is Southern's freight No. 51, powered by a big, handsome Ms-4 class heavy Mikado, No. 4821, had finished working the Dundee yard; however, before girding itself in order to take on Cemetery Hill, the crew stopped at Danville's passenger station to fill its tender with water in order to make sure it would have enough steam to win the coming battle. The fireman crawled over the coal and had the water spout placed in the tender when this photo was made this cloudy, hot July 14, 1948 afternoon.

Here is one opponent preparing for the fight; the standard steam motive power for the Southern's main line, with 59,600 lbs. of tractive effort and 63" drivers ready for the bout with its adversary: Cemetery Hill. With a great deal of "shotgunning" exhaust, flying cinders, rods clanking, No. 4821 would get its tonnage out of the station, over the hill and on to its next stop in Greensboro, N. C.

To see and hear such a titanic struggle of steam vs. gravity was thrilling, exhilarating and memorable. It was an event that once seen and heard, you would never ever forget this rail drama!

Photographer, Ray Carneal; Curt Tillotson Collection.

No. 4824 (Ms-4 class heavy 2-8-2): drivers, 63"; engine weight, 326,000 lbs.; steam pressure, 200 lbs.; tractive effort, 59,600 lbs.; superheated; Richmond built, 1923; tender weight (loaded with 10,000 gal. of water and 16 tons of coal); 191,400 lbs.; engine & tender length, 83' 1/16"; engine height, 14'11"; Worthington feedwater heater; Standard stoker; Hodges trailer trucks; retired, Aug. of 1953 (sold to the Baltimore Steel Co.).

One of the hardest assignments a crew on the Southern's Greensboro-Goldsboro, N. C. line could receive in early 1950 was to work No. 74 and No. 75 because, unlike the through freights such as No.'s 252, 253, 254 and 255, these two freights could be classified as main line locals since they worked almost every station along the 130-mile run-many which were not served by the through runs. Indeed, it usually required 8-10 hours, or even longer, to complete all the work necessary to keep the Southern customers happy.

This Jan. 20, 1950 afternoon, we find No. 75 completing its work at the East Durham, N. C. yard. Shown pulling out its last cut of cars, passing over the Ellis Road crossing and entering the main line was the big Ms-4 class heavy 2-8-2, No. 4824 (notice that huge Worthington feedwater heater above the No. 3 and No. 4 drivers) with the engine's stoker and sanders on. Soon, once all the cars were on the main line, the brakeman would close the switch so that No. 75 would back its cars towards the remainder of its train, make a brake test and then leave town, heading west to work another town on its way to Greensboro. It left Goldsboro at 5:30 a.m. this cold but sunny day. And the westbounder finally departed East Durham at 1:30 p.m.

Since there was a coaling tower, water tower and other engine facilities at East Durham (behind the photographer), along with an 0-6-0 switcher plus the beginning of the East Durham to Oxford, Henderson, N. C. and Keysville, Va. branch of the Richmond Division, East Durham (located on the Southern's Danville Division), was one of the busiest yards on the entire line. Indeed, No. 4824 received coal and water at this location before leaving town.

Today, the main line remains much the same as it was in 1950, although it now has 132 lbs. continuous rail. A switcher still works the yard and the area's customers but practically all the other facilities have been removed. Now the Greensboro-Cary, N. C. portion of the line has C.T.C. and there are four Amtrak passenger trains plus numerous freights that keep the big, big rails very shiny.

Even with the increased business, C.T.C. and other modern appurtenances-all designed to make it a very efficient part of the Norfolk Southern-no train movements today could ever make the drama shown here this cold day in early 1950 as No. 75 put on a spectacular exit that only the "iron horse" could create. The looks, sounds and smells were outstanding, something none of the massive six-axle diesel "monsters" will never be able to reproduce. That's for sure!

*Credit: Photographer, Ray Carneal; Curt Tillotson Collection.*

No. 4839 (Ms-4 class heavy 2-8-2): drivers, 63"; engine weight, 326,000 lbs.; steam pressure, 200 lbs.; tractive effort, 59,600 lbs.; superheated; Richmond built, 1923; tender weight (loaded with 10,000 gal. of water and 16 tons of coal); 191,400 lbs.; engine & tender length, 83' 1/16"; engine height, 14'11"; Worthington feedwater heater; Standard stoker; Hodges trailer trucks; retired, Oct. 17, 1952 (sold to the Baltimore Steel Co.).

Ah, the main line, where anything can come along at anytime! A case in point is shown here in Raleigh, N. C. on a cold but sunny (and exciting) afternoon in Feb. of 1947.

A long string of cars were placed on the Southern's connection track at Selma, N. C. by the Atlantic Coast Line earlier in the day. Since the tonnage left by the ACL was too much for the next regularly scheduled freight to handle without using a doubleheader for motive power, the Southern decided to get these cars to Spencer Yard (via Greensboro, N. C.) ASAP!

As a result, we have an opportunity to see a big, graphite covered, white wheeled, clean Ms-4 heavy 2-8-2, No. 4839, gaining speed-upgrade-out of Raleigh with the sights and sounds that could only be made by a Southern 4800 series "Mike"-in a hurry!

Extra 4839 West is passing through Raleigh's Pullen Park and ready to head by my "alma mater"-NC State College (now NC State University). To this day, I'll never understand how I was able to earn my BA degree from this excellent university since there were so many "distractions" as shown here. Of course, my "distractions" were diesel powered but they were still most exhilarating "distractions."

There were 35 cars in the Extra West's consist this glorious afternoon when steam still ruled both the Southern and Seaboard Air Line. The Southern and SAL met in Raleigh and formed a section of double track from Boylan Tower (in the background, down the hill) to Cary, N. C.-approximately 8

No. 4819 (Ms-4 class heavy 2-8-2): drivers, 63"; engine weight, 326,000 lbs.; steam pressure, 200 lbs.; tractive effort, 59,600 lbs.; superheated; Richmond built, 1923; tender weight (loaded with 10,000 gal. of water and 16 tons of coal); 191,400 lbs.; engine & tender length, 83' 1/16"; engine height, 14'11"; Worthington feedwater heater; Standard stoker; Hodges trailer trucks; retired, Oct. 17, 1952 (scrapped at Haynes-Spartanburg, S. C.).

The only action in the little community of Motley, Va. was (and remains) trains, trains, trains-my kind of place to be!

Southern's No. 56 passes the only rail structure in this area, which is 5 miles south of Altavista, Va. with a big burly Ms-4 class heavy Mikado, No. 4819, pulling 40 cars on a late afternoon in Oct. of 1950, doing a good 40-45 m.p.h. downgrade. Notice the white rails beside No. 4819: there is a stiff grade out of Altavista and a great deal of sanding is required to get the tonnage south.

The Danville Division freight had only one stop to be made before the crew, which pulled out of Spencer (N.C.) Yard earlier this morning, could get a rest. Once out of Lynchburg, Va.'s Montview Yard, No. 56 would only have another 8 miles to travel before No. 4819 and its train would arrive at the historic rail town of Monroe, Va. where there was, among other rail facilities, a railroad Y.M.C.A. for the crews arriving there.

Today, this area is covered with trees, kudzu, weeds and bushes; you could not make an exposure at this location. There are two reasons why this is so. First, during the steam era, there were section crews who were responsible for track maintenance over a few miles of track. These crews not only made sure that the track(s) in their sections remained in excellent condition; they also kept the right-of-way clean. And secondly, the cinders spewed out of the steam locomotives covered the ground so deeply that grass and other plants could not grow. This will help explain why the Southern's right-of-way remained so clean and clear until the arrival of the diesels and track maintenance was handled by machines-a good example of what happens when you lose the "human touch."

*Credit: Photographer, Hugh Stafford Bryant, Jr.; Curt Tillotson Collection.*

miles away. Today, the tracks are still there and they are kept busy by the trains of the NS, CSX and Amtrak. Notice how the rails of the westbound main were very white-caused by the sanding of thousands of trains over several decades of working up the long grade out of Raleigh-they are still white to this day. At Cary, the SAL's main line from Richmond to Miami headed south while the Southern headed west to Greensboro and the Washington-Atlanta main line.

Man, those were the days! Thank goodness for main lines!

*Credit: Photographer, Wiley Bryan; Curt Tillotson Collection*

No. 4819 (Ms-4 class heavy 2-8-2): drivers, 63"; engine weight, 326,000 lbs.; steam pressure, 200 lbs.; tractive effort, 59,600 lbs.; superheated; Richmond built, 1923; tender weight (loaded with 10,000 gal. of water and 16 tons of coal); 191,400 lbs.; engine & tender length, 83' 1/16"; engine height, 14'11"; Worthington feedwater heater; Standard stoker; Hodges trailer trucks; retired, Oct.17, 1952 (scrapped at Haynes-Spartanburg, S.C.).

Arriving at the south end of Lynchburg, Va.'s Montview Yard, Southern's No. 56, powered by a handsome Ms-4 class heavy 2-8-2, No. 4819, is slowing its speed in preparation to pick up and set off cars before heading on to Monroe, Va. (approximately 8 miles to the north) where the crew members would have a chance to have a rest at the rail YMCA, located just behind the Monroe station/yard office.

You can see, about 8 cars back from No. 4819, that the head end brakeman had already dropped off the engine in order to uncouple the train's Lynchburg cars. It's a late afternoon in Aug. of 1950 (5:15 p.m.) and soon the sun would set. The big Ms-4 would arrive in Monroe after dark since it would spend nearly an hour working Montview Yard.

Notice how clean the grounds around the south end of the yard appears. Also, all tracks looked in excellent condition. This is a good example of what the difference between the "human touch" vs. the machine when it comes to track and roadway maintenance really meant. The machines are less expensive but when people were involved, it really showed-as it did in this photo.

It's 1950 and more and more of the main line freights-and passenger runs-were powered by the diesel-electrics. As a result, such pleasing scenes as this were becoming rare. On this particular afternoon, however, it would be hard to believe that the days of this Worthington feedwater equipped, heavy Ms-4 and its other steam family members were numbered. Still, that time will come in the near future, so let's enjoy the arrival of No. 56, pulled by No. 4819, in the "City of Seven Hills."

The looks, the sounds and even the smells were great. The engine was still clean, even after the 158-mile trip from Spencer, N.C. were the roundhouse "boys" had cleaned up No. 4819 before it took No. 56 north: that was how things were done on the Southern during the days of steam.

*Credit: Photographer, H. Stafford Bryant, Jr.; Curt Tillotson Collection.*

No. 4833 (Ms-4 class heavy 2-8-2): driver, 63"; engine weight, 326,000 lbs.; steam pressure, 200 lbs.; tractive effort, 59,600 lbs.; superheated; Richmond built, 1923; tender weight (loaded with 10,000 gal. of water and 16 tons of coal); 191,400 lbs.; engine & tender length, 83' 1/16"; engine height, 14'11"; Worthington feedwater heater; Standard stoker; Hodges trailer trucks; retired, Nov. of 1952 (sold to the Baltimore Steel Co.).

Monroe, Va.-now that's a name most all serious railfans are familiar with. Probably the first image that comes to mind at the mention of this location would be the wreck of Southern's fast mail train No. 97 in 1903. As a result of this wreck, which occurred north of Danville, Va., one of the most famous rail songs was created: "The Wreck of Old 97," which begins with the lyrics: "They gave him his orders in Monroe, Virginia..."

Most railfans in the southeast, however, did not need to hear that song to conjure up the mystic of Monroe. This was a 100% rail town on the Southern's Washington-Atlanta main line. Facilities found in this famous vicinity included: a large yard, roundhouse, turntable, a station which contained the yardmasters, dispatchers, and division officers (Monroe was the end of the Danville Division which began in Salisbury, N.C. and the beginning of the Washington Division-165 miles north to Washington Union Station. There was also a railroad YMCA located behind the station where the crews from Salisbury and Washington-Alexandria could have a bath, good food, and a soft bed to rest on before returning to their home base.

On the ready track, shown here this hot and humid morning on June 30, 1949, were the two classes of main line steam motive power for both freight and passenger trains: on the right was a big, dependable Southern Ms-4 class heavy 2-8-2 (No. 4833) which was scheduled to take an extra freight out of town. Behind the impressive "Mike" was the green and gold colored Elesco feedwater heater equipped, elegant and memorable Ps-4 heavy Pacific (No. 1394) which was shiny, its wheels trimmed in white along with its cylinder heads, walkways and even the bottom of the cowcatcher and ready for a passenger assignment. Hey, what's that green, white and gold colored motive power shown behind the Ps-4? Someone said it was a "diesel"-an F-7 model-whatever that was. Oh well, let's concentrate on those well-maintained, super clean freight and passenger movers.

This was Monroe where, by 1949, there were over 50 freight and a dozen passenger trains that stopped, changed crews-and, on occasion, a change in engines-every 24 hours. This was truly a "sacred" rail location for all those who loved trains. I visited Monroe on three occasions and was never disappointed in finding exciting rail action.

Today, there is nothing-absolutely nothing-at what used to be Monroe: no yard, no roundhouse, no station, no YMCA-absolutely nothing! All the facilities at Monroe were transferred to Lynchburg, Va.'s Montview Yard. There only remains a sign, located where the station used to be, which had the name, "Monroe" on both sides; however, there is nothing to remind you of the railroad town that became part of the lexicon of the rail world-nothing!

Progress: it's not always as great as some maintain!

*Credit: Photographer, H. Stafford Bryant, Jr.; Curt Tillotson Collection.*

No. 4829 (Ms-4 class heavy 2-8-2): drivers, 63"; engine weight, 326,000 lbs.; steam pressure, 200 lbs.; tractive effort, 59,600 lbs.; superheated; Richmond built, 1923; tender weight (loaded with 10,000 gal. of water and 16 tons of coal); 191,400 lbs.; engine & tender length, 83' 1/16"; engine height, 14'11"; Worthington feedwater heater; Standard stoker; Hodges trailer trucks; retired, April of 1952 (sold to the Baltimore Steel Co.).

Snow and trains will automatically result in a smile on the face of a railfan. However, if you make that a steam locomotive plus snow, that smile would not only be on your face but in your heart and soul as well, for this "human-like" machine in action, in the snow, would guarantee you a wonderful memory never forgotten.

It was approximately 8:35 a.m. on a cold morning in Alexandria, Va. as Southern's "hot shot," No. 153, is shown departing the area, heading towards Monroe, Va. and points south in a style that could only be created by a steam engine such as this big, handsome Ms-4 class heavy 2-8-2, No. 4829, in Jan. of 1939. By this time, the Ms-4 was Southern's standard main line motive power for moving freights. And the Southern crews made sure that No. 4829 was clean, had its smoke box and cylinder heads covered in graphite; its driving rods were as polished as those of the colorful Ps-4's, for the road's reputation for having the cleanest motive power-in good operational condition-would be maintained (it was!).

Alexandria, Va. was the place to be if you wanted a large volume of train movements to photograph. By World War II, it was not unusual to have over 150 trains entering and leaving this location. Just 2-3 miles to the north was the vital Potomac Yard. All the trains of the Southern's Washington-Atlanta main line, the RF&P's line from Richmond, Va. (which included the vast number of trains from the Seaboard and the Atlantic Coast line) plus the trains of the C&O (which used the rails of the Southern from Orange, Va.) — all these movements into and out of "Pot Yard" created a volume of rail action so great that it was rarely duplicated elsewhere.

Indeed, during WWII, army personnel with loaded weapons, were stationed near this important vicinity where the rail traffic moved from the South to the North-and vice versa-in order to protect it from possible sabotage. Soldiers were also found at both ends of the bridge, called the "Long Bridge," which spanned the Potomac River, to protect this extremely important double track structure from possible enemy activity.

There were so many trains entering and leaving this area that the railroad companies involved had a four-track main line established. The two tracks on the east side were used by freights entering and departing "Pot Yard" while the double track on the west side accommodated the large number of passenger runs to and from Washington Union Station.

Throw in snow with a four-track main line that supports 100+ trains and you have a location dreamed about by railfans who never visited the area around "Alex." It was one of those locations that you had to see it to truly believe it. I was fortunate to visit "Alex" on three occasions in the mid-1970s. There were over 20 passenger trains listed on the schedule board at the station, with the Southern's magnificent "Southern Crescent," being the only non-Amtrak varnish to visit each day. And there were freights, freights, freights! On one visit, I arrived at Alexandria near 7:30 a.m. and remained in the vicinity until 7:45 p.m. During that time period, I photographed over 30 trains! During the steam era, the volume of rail traffic was almost unbelievable.

A clean Southern Ms-4 powered freight, picking up speed-in the surrounding snow-was an ideal way to start a railfan's day. Wouldn't you agree?

*Credit: Photographer, Collection of C. W. Witbeck; Curt Tillotson Collection.*

No. 6350 (Ms-4 class heavy 2-8-2): drivers, 63"; engine weight, 326,000 lbs.; steam pressure, 200 lbs.; tractive effort, 59,600 lbs.; superheated; Baldwin built, 1928; tender weight (loaded with 10,000 gal. of water and 16 tons of coal); 191,400 lbs.; engine & tender length, 83' 1/16"; engine height, 14'11"; Elesco feedwater heater; Standard stoker; Hodges trailer trucks; retired, June 8, 1953 (scrapped at Finley, Alabama).

An Elesco feedwater heater equipped Southern Ms-4 class heavy Mikado pulling a long freight at speed with the stoker opened, on a well-kept main line, on a clean, elevated curve and the late afternoon sunlight highlighting the entire engine-especially the running gear: these were all the ingredients necessary to make an outstanding, unforgettable exposure. And, thankfully, a railfan/photographer was nearby to record on film this memorable drama, one that truly represented the Southern, in action, during the age of steam.

It was a cold Feb. afternoon in 1949 near Powder Spring, Ga. as Extra 6350 South came into view, whipping around the curve at a good 50+ m.p.h., pulling this extra freight from Chattanooga to Atlanta (approximately 23 miles away). And, if you needed an extra item to enhance this already thrilling portrait of steam on the move, the heavy, dependable 2-8-2 was shown passing a semaphore signal at the north end of a pass track.

I'm not sure if the engineer spotted the photographer and told his fireman to cut on the stoker or if the fireman just needed more steam to keep his engine's pressure at the required 200-lb. level. For whatever reason, that volume of smoke added that last touch that would make this one of the most dramatic representations of an Ms-4 class 2-8-2 doing what it was designed to do and it also helped to explain why the Southern decided to make the Ms-4 class "Mikes" the standard main line freight motive power and it remained so until the arrival of the diesel-electric locomotive.

Admittedly, seeing four FT units coming around this same curve under the same circumstances described earlier would be an exciting sight. However, the diesel (which had practically all its main parts inside its car body) could never EVER produce the action of a steam locomotive (with most of its working parts outside the engine cover), working at full throttle with the stoker on, making good time on good track! Indeed, in the "looks" department, there was no comparison between the two forms of motive power. The diesel might have been more efficient but the steam locomotive could do the same job with far more "enthusiasm."

*Credit: Photographer, R. D. Sharpless; Curt Tillotson Collection.*

No. 6321 (Ms-4 class heavy 2-8-2): drivers, 63"; engine weight, 326,000 lbs.; steam pressure, 200 lbs.; tractive effort, 59,600 lbs.; superheated; Richmond built, 1926; tender weight (loaded with 10,000 gal. of water and 16 tons of coal); 191,400 lbs.; engine & tender length, 83' 1/16"; engine height, 14'11"; Elesco feedwater heater; Standard stoker; Hodges trailer trucks; retired, July of 1959 (sold to David J. Joseph).

During the steam era when the Southern purchased locomotives, they assigned them to certain divisions or other parts of their system. For example, once a group of new engines arrived on the property, some could be assigned to the Danville or Charlotte Divisions or the CNO&TP, the AGS, etc. Once the division received their locomotives, the division's name would be painted under the engine's number on each side of the locomotive's cab. If ever you have an opportunity to visit the Smithsonian Institute's Museum of Science and Technology, look at that magnificent Ps-4 heavy Pacific, No. 1401. Under the engine number on the cab you will find the name, "Charlotte," painted in gold. No. 1401 spent many years on the Southern's Charlotte Division. Indeed, when the Southern ferried the body of President Franklin D. Roosevelt north to Washington, D. C. in April of 1945, No. 1401 was the lead Ps-4 of the double-headed train between Greenville, S. C. and Salisbury, N. C. This was the territory of the Charlotte Division (north end).

Once the diesels began replacing steam locomotives, the steamers remaining went into a passenger or freight pool. From 1949 through 1953, it was not unusual to find a locomotive originally assigned to the CNO&TP operating on the Danville Division or anywhere on the road.

In this photo, we find a beautiful Southern Ms-4 heavy Mikado, No. 6321, working at full throttle up a grade (notice the different colors of the rails), pulling this southbound extra freight south of Danville, Ky. On a partly cloudy morning in July of 1939. The big "girl's" tender was still full of coal so it was not far out of Danville, carrying the tonnage towards Chattanooga. It was an engine assigned to the CNO&TP and was photographed at work on the CNO&TP.

No. 6321 had just passed under "tell tails" (located two cars behind the hard working 2-8-2). Since the Ms-4 was approaching a highway overpass, the Southern had placed these "tell tails" on both sides of the main line (and on both sides of the bridge) to warn a brakeman or any other member of the crew that could be riding the roof of a freight car, that a low overhead bridge (or tunnel) was nearby, so he (or they) should get off the roof or at least "duck!" Today, however, there are no walkways on top of most cars, so the "tell tails" went the way of the steam locomotive.

Boy, No. 6321 was really "barking" with "snappy" and loud stack talk; its stoker and sanders were on as well. The heavy 2-8-2 was down to 15-10 m.p.h., using every bit of its 59,600 lbs. of tractive effort to get the tonnage to its destination. Its "blasting" was so loud, so violent, that the railroad placed a sheet of metal on the bottom of the overhead bridges-called "blast plates"-in order to prevent any damage to the structure, especially in an area that had a grade passing under it.

This was the dramatic, the exciting and thrilling railroading, steam style. THIS type of action helped make a person a railfan for life. It was a machine, true, but it acted as if it was alive! Ask any old "hogger" who worked on a steamer and he will tell you that each locomotive had its own personality. And you had to learn what that personality was in order to have a successful run.

Yep, once seeing and hearing such action as depicted here, you became a railfan!

*Photographer, Unknown; Curt Tillotson Collection.*

No. 4861 and No. 4905 (Ms-4 class heavy 2-8-2's): drivers, 63" (both); engine weight, 326,000 lbs. (both); steam pressure, 200 lbs.(both); tractive effort, 59,600 lbs. (both); superheated (both); Schenectady built, 1924 (No. 4861) and Baldwin built, 1928 (No. 4905); tender weight (loaded with 10,000 gal. of water and 16 tons of coal); 191,400 lbs. (both); Elesco feedwater heater (both); Standard stoker (both); retired, Oct. of 1952 (No. 4861-sold to the Baltimore Steel Co.) and Dec. of 1952 (No. 4905).

Two Southern Elesco feedwater heater equipped Ms-4 heavy 2-8-2's departing Atlanta's Inman Yard with a vengeance; wide-opened, stokers on, with the fireman on the second engine clearing his cylinder cocks, in the smoke and fury of fire, steam and steel vs. the pull of the tonnage tied to the rear of the two, thundering Mikados moving a westbound extra freight towards Birmingham in a scene that simply had to be seen to be believed. What more could a railfan want?

The extra west, headed by No. 4905 (with the help of No. 4861), had over 70 cars in tow on this dreary day (weather-wise only) in Feb. of 1947, as the two "Mikes" put on a show that the vast majority of railfans could only dream of experiencing personally. And just think, this was a common occurrence when steam ruled the rails!

Look at the rails supporting this drama. They were as white as those found on Saluda Grade. However, the heavy sanding of the numerous freights leaving Inman Yard-in a hurry-could cause the same effects on the twin strips of steel as the sanding found on the grueling climb up Saluda Grade.

When looking at such a sight (frozen in time on film), how do you capture the sounds, the smells, the trembling on the ground; two crews working as one-without radio communication-just how can you put all of this soul stirring action into words that would adequately describe such an event? You can't! You really had to be there for the special moment to have a chance to set into your mind so that you would be able to savor the dramatic happening for yourself. So, since it would be impossible to capture the essence of this magnificent display of steam power into words, I'll just say: look at the photo and allow your imagination to do the rest. It was truly a rail event at its "steamy" best!

*Credit: Photographer, Unknown; Curt Tillotson Collection.*

No. 6332 (Ms-4 class heavy 2-8-2): drivers, 63"; engine weight, 326,000 lbs.; steam pressure, 200 lbs.; tractive effort, 59,600 lbs.; superheated; Richmond built, 1926; tender weight (loaded with 10,000 gal. of water and 16 tons of coal); 191,400 lbs.; engine & tender length, 83' 1/16"; engine height, 14'11"; Elesco feedwater heater; Standard stoker; Hodges trailer trucks; retired, May of 1953 (scrapped at Finley, Alabama).

During World War II, the United States sent a tremendous amount of supplies to Great Britain to help defeat the Axis powers. This was especially true for fuel: oil, gas, etc. As one officer said, "Oil is blood!" Tanker after tanker would leave from several ports on the Gulf of Mexico, loaded with fuel, head up the east coast to New York City, where they would form a convoy and, with warships providing some protection, they would head out across the dangerous Atlantic Ocean where German submarines waited to try and destroy them.

Because so many tankers were sunk by German "U-boats" along our coast, most refineries began using the railroads, sending solid "tank trains" to New York and other ports. These special trains were 1st class, priority runs which did not take the siding for any other trains. They were providing the fuel for the armies of the democracies to help keep the world free from the demonic side of life.

We find such a train on the Southern's CNO&TP depicted here. Extra 6332 North had over 50 cars. The precious fuel in tow near New River, TN this June afternoon in 1945, heading towards Cincinnati-218 miles north.

You could tell that this Southern Ms-4 heavy Mikado was running on the CNO&TP for two reasons. First, the 2-8-2's number-No. 6332-was a "Mike" originally assigned to this rugged and busy area. And secondly, the big and handsome engine was equipped with a Wimble duct (placed on top of the engine's steam and sand domes). The CNO&TP featured an area known as the "Rat Hole." It was a section of track where there were over 20 tunnels-many of them narrow, long and on a grade. In the early years, many engine crews were nearly asphyxiated with the smoke and fumes coming back into their cabs while in one of those "holes." Also, the blasting of the engines knocked rocks off the top of the tunnels. The Wimble smoke deflector was added to all engines traveling through this infamous area. When approaching a tunnel, the engineer would activate a switch which would move the deflector over the engine's smokestack and this would channel the smoke back over the cab, thereby saving the crews and it also protected the top of the tunnels. The freight engines had a long Wimble duct while the passenger locomotives usually had a short smoke deflector since they went through the tunnels at a much faster pace.

Notice the blade on the semaphore signal was on its way down after being in a vertical position (indicating a "clear" track). As the extra north passed by, the signal "arm" began to drop to a horizontal mode (this was a "stop" indication).

The American railroads carried over 95% of the soldiers and the war goods which were necessary to defeat our enemies. The Southern had more military bases located on their lines than any other railroad in our nation. And, as a result, it needed any and all engines that could operate to move the almost unbelievable amount of tonnage. For railfans of Southern steam power, it enabled "us" to see steam in action far longer than the Southern had planned. The road had decided to completely dieselize its entire fleet of motive power by 1940; however, the demands of the war-and for a few years after our great victory-delayed the road's plans which were finally completed on June 17, 1953 in Chattanooga when the last regularly assigned steam run was completed.

The photographer did an outstanding job recording, this "tank train" in action. He could have been arrested as a possible enemy saboteur if any soldiers or law officers had been nearby. Thank goodness, this did not happen for we are fortunate that he was lucky and made this excellent exposure.

*Credit: Photographer, Doyle Inman; Curt Tillotson Collection.*

No. 4881 (Ms-4 class heavy 2-8-2): drivers, 63"; engine weight, 326,000 lbs.; steam pressure, 200 lbs.; tractive effort, 59,600 lbs.; superheated; Richmond built, 1926; tender weight (loaded with 10,000 gal. of water and 16 tons of coal); 191,400 lbs.; engine & tender length, 83' 1/16"; engine height, 14'11"; Elesco feedwater heater; Standard stoker; Hodges trailer trucks; retired, Nov. of 1952 (sold to the Baltimore Steel Co.).

The 2nd section of through freight No. 54 is shown negotiating a super-elevated curve near Powder Springs, Ga. on a run from Atlanta to Chattanooga this March 14, 1948 at 2:30 p.m.-just 23 miles north of Atlanta. A Southern big, burly and yet, esthetically pleasing Ms-4 class heavy 2-8-2, No. 4881, was leading the second of three sections of this freight in the grand style that only a steam locomotive could produce.

The roundhouse crew in Atlanta made sure "their" Ms-4 was "presentable" before it left town: the engine was washed until its jacket and tender were shiny clean, white paint was applied to No. 4881's walkways, the bottom of its cowcatcher-even the "push pole" sections were a brilliant white-as was the rims of the pony trucks but not its drivers (?). And with that impressive Elesco feedwater heater in front of its smokestack, one can see why a vast number of railfans rated these engines as the most popular freights movers not only on the Southern but, arguably, on any other roads as well (I agree with this opinion 100%).

Passing through two semaphore signals, the one on the left, had its blade in the vertical position when No. 4881 was approaching-this was a "clear signal" indication. Once the big freight "hog" passed, the blade began to drop to the "stop" position-like the signal to the right of the train. Soon the modern automatic block, three colored signals will replace the old semaphores.

By 1948, this was still the picture of modern railroading at its best on the Southern. However, by 1953, the modern and admired road would be completely dieselized. And then this same train (No. 54) would be photographed at this location with "growlers" as the motive power. As a result, I'm glad that Mr. Inman was there with his camera this afternoon in '48, so he could give us a glimpse of what it was like when the Ms-4's and Ps-4's ruled the rails in that wonderful, colorful and exciting era of steam power.

*Credit: Photographer, R. D. Sharpless; Curt Tillotson Collection.*

No. 6360 (Ms-4 class heavy 2-8-2): drivers, 63"; engine weight, 326,000 lbs.; steam pressure, 200 lbs.; tractive effort, 59,600 lbs.; superheated; Baldwin built, 1928; tender weight (loaded with 10,000 gal. of water and 16 tons of coal); 191,400 lbs.; engine & tender length, 83' 1/16"; engine height 14'11"; Elesco feedwater heater; Standard stoker; Hodges trailer trucks; retired, Nov. of 1952 (sold to the Baltimore Steel Co.).

A Southern heavy Mikado, No. 6360, wide-opened, working upgrade, using every bit of its 59,600 lbs. of tractive effort to get this southbound extra freight to its destination while passing through the infamous area of the Southern's CNO&TP called the "Rat Hole," with a display of raw power.

Between Danville, Ky. and Harriman, Tn. (approximately 142 miles), there were over 20 tunnels (some with narrow clearances, some short and some long and many of them were located on a grade). To help overcome the horrible and dangerous conditions within these tunnels, with the engines at full throttle, the Southern equipped practically all its freight and passenger power, which worked through this area, with the effective Wimble duct-a smoke deflector which was placed on the top of the locomotive's steam and sand domes. When nearing one of these bores, the engineer would activate a switch which would cause the duct to move forward, covering its smokestack. The duct would divert the smoke over the engine cab, protecting the crew from possible asphyxiation and also save the roof of the tunnels form the blasting effects of the "shot-gunning" locomotives. Since passenger engines moved at a much faster pace, most were fitted with a shorter deflector.

Over the years, the Southern tried several types of steam power to move the tonnage through this area: the 2-8-0 Consolidations could only pull just so much tonnage even when doubleheaded, while the massive 2-10-2's were far too large and caused damage to the tunnel roofs with their enormous and violent exhaust. Finally, the Ms-4 heavy 2-8-2's proved to be a good engine for the "Rat Hole"-which no longer exists since the Southern eliminated most of the tunnels and enlarged the ones that remain; the road "straightened out" the line, making it a most efficient section of the CNO&TP without any restrictions. This work was completed in Jan. of 1963 and cost $35 million dollars.

It was a very cold day in Jan. of 1945 with snow on the surrounding hills-along with several inches of cinders along the right-of-way when Extra 6360 south was photographed, blasting by heading towards Chattanooga. Look at how white No. 6360's driver wheels appeared. A great deal of sanding could not only discolor the rails, it could also turn an engine's running gear just as white as well.

The sounds of this hard-working "Mike" were tremendous! I can imagine its fireman was glad that his big "girl" was equipped with the reliable Standard stoker to help him keep the 2-8-2's steam pressure at the required 200 lb. mark so it would work at its maximum ability.

The "Rat Hole" area was a costly piece of railroad to operate; but, for the railfans, it was a wondrous area to view and photograph Southern's best steam power working "all-out"-what a sight, what a sound, what a railroad!

*Credit: Photographer, Doyle Inman; Curt Tillotson Collection.*

No. 6369 (Ms-4 class heavy 2-8-2): drivers, 63"; engine weight, 326,000 lbs.; steam pressure, 200 lbs.; tractive effort, 59,600 lbs.; superheated; Baldwin built, 1928; tender weight (loaded with 10,000 gal. of water and 16 tons of coal); 191,400 lbs.; engine & tender length, 83' 1/16"; engine height, 14'11"; Elesco feedwater heater; Standard stoker; Hodges trailer trucks; retired, Nov. of 1952 (sold to the Baltimore Steel Co.).

As a result of the sinking of many loaded tankers moving up the east coast by German submarines during World War II, the U.S. government decided to use railroads as one of the main forms of transportation to get the precious fuel to the northeastern ports for shipment, by convoy, to Europe.

The Southern carried the vast majority of these solid "tank trains"-loads north, empties south on both its Washington-Atlanta and CNO&TP main lines. These extra movements had priority over all other trains. And, during most of the war, the military protected several key points along these routes of the "tank trains" to make sure they reached their destinations safely.

Shown in this outstanding photo was one of these "hot shots" moving thousands of gallons of fuel north, pulled by a big, handsome Southern Ms-4 heavy 2-8-2, No. 6369, pictured making good time (notice how the Mikado's smoke tends to drift back, close to the cars-a sure sign of speed) across one of the most photographed locations on the CNO&TP; the long, narrow bridge over the Cumberland River near Burnside, Ky. (165 miles south of Cincinnati) this beautiful day in 1944.

At the north end of the bridge, all northbound trains immediately plunged into one of the many tunnels found on the "Rat Hole" portion of the CNO&TP. Actually, most exposures were taken of southbound trains, emerging from the tunnel and entering the bridge, from the hills overlooking the main line. Indeed, the most famous photograph made was taken of the first FT-model diesels-No. 6100 and three mates-in 1941. Leaning out of the cab window of No. 6100 in the exposure was fireman Charles F. Denny who, unfortunately, died at the battle of Okinawa while he served as a Marine private.

As a point of interest, today this entire area is under over one hundred feet of water! A dam was built nearby, creating a huge reservoir of water. As a result of this government project, the Southern had to build several miles of new track plus a huge, double-track, photogenic bridge-all keeping the CNO&TP's impressive volume of trains moving.

Here is a prime example of the importance of railroads both in times of peace and war: they can move almost anything, anywhere, in all types of weather, efficiently and dependably!

*Credit: Photographer, Doyle Inman; Curt Tillotson Collection.*

No. 6323 (Ms-4 class heavy 2-8-2): driver, 63"; engine weight, 326,000 lbs.; steam pressure, 200 lbs.; tractive effort, 59,600 lbs.; superheated; Richmond built, 1926; tender weight (loaded with 10,000 gal. of water and 16 tons of coal); 191,400 lbs.; engine & tender length, 83' 1/16"; engine height, 14'11"; Elesco feedwater heater; Standard stoker; Hodges trailer trucks; retired, Aug. of 1954 (sold to David J. Joseph).

The winter months, even with the cold and other adverse conditions, offered the railfans opportunities to view and photograph excellent action of steam locomotives at work. The atmosphere was free of the humidity and smog. As a result, your photos would be very sharp and clear-far more so than during the heat of summertime. There was very little undergrowth near track side to interfere with selecting a good location to take your exposures of the "iron horse" passing by. Indeed, the winter season enabled you to have more areas than could be found during the growing part of the year in order to indulge your love of this "human-like" machine, pulling the nation's passenger and freight. And, most importantly, with the cold weather around, it almost always guaranteed you a good smoke effect as the steamer passed by you and your camera. Even if the engine's stoker was not on, the hot exhaust of the engine meeting the extreme cold atmosphere would give you a white volume of smoke (actually it was condensation). And if the stoker was on, you had both black and white exhaust rolling out of the locomotive's smokestack in a glorious fashion.

This photo will allow you to see why the winter period was a great time for a railfan. Here we have Southern's No. 55, pulled by the husky looking but esthetically pleasing Ms-4 heavy Mikado, No. 6323, near Oneida, Tn. In Feb. of 1946, on a run from Cincinnati (209 miles to the north) to Chattanooga (128 miles to the south). With snow on the ground and the fireman's stoker on, look at that beautiful smoke effect rolling out of this Elesco feedwater heater equipped "Mike!"

With that Wimble duct smoke deflector placed on top of No. 6323's steam and sand domes, you could make a guess that freight No. 55 was on the Southern's CNO&TP-and you would be correct. You'll also notice the different colors of the rails. No. 6323's fireman had the coal gong into the big 2-8-2's firebox via his stoker since the southbounder was working upgrade.

Everything about this photo seemed to be so right: snow on the right-of-way, semaphore signals, double track and that wonderful Mikado at work, helping to put more funds into the Southern's coffers.

True, the winter months could present many obstacles for railfans; however, in many incidences-such as this photo showing this handsome 2-8-2 in action-these problems were overlooked when you could make an outstanding photo such as the one depicted, which enabled us to view steam power in such dramatic action.

*Credit: Photographer, Doyle Inman; Curt Tillotson Collection.*

No. 6367 (Ms-4 class heavy 2-8-2): drivers, 63"; engine weight, 326,000 lbs.; steam pressure, 200 lbs.; tractive effort, 59,600 lbs.; superheated; Baldwin built, 1928; tender weight (loaded with 10,000 gal. of water and 16 tons of coal); 191,400 lbs.; engine & tender length, 83' 1/16"; engine height, 14'11"; Elesco feedwater heater; Standard stoker; Hodges trailer trucks; retired, Nov. of 1952 (sold to the Baltimore Steel Co.).

A train on a bridge, especially one with steam power at the headend, always produced a most dramatic setting for a photographer. This exposure was no exception to this fact. In this instance, we find a Southern Ms-4 class heavy Mikado, No. 6367-the standard main line freight power on the road before the arrival of the diesel-pulling an extra southbound freight near Dallas, Ga.-approximately 34 miles north of Atlanta-doing a good 50+ m.p.h. with a clear stack (darn it) after leaving Chattanooga (back 118 miles to the north) this afternoon in Oct. of 1948.

This photogenic structure spanned the Pumpkin Vine Creek (I kid you not), a bridge visited on several occasions each and every day and night since it was located on the vital main line between Atlanta and Chattanooga.

Even though the big and powerful No. 6367 had been on the road for several hours, it was still clean and most impressive-a trait associated (and justly so) with the Southern whose crews always felt that each and every engine-big or small-was a member of their family and were cared for accordingly. Indeed, before heading back to Chattanooga with a freight, the "boys" at Atlanta's Inman Yard would make sure the 2-8-2 would be thoroughly washed, graphite would be added to its smoke box and a judicious amount of white trim would be placed on its walkways, cowcatcher, driver and pony truck rims. Then it would be loaded with "grade A" coal plus good water plus its sand dome would be filled with fine material that would help the "Mike" maintain traction with the rails, especially when working upgrade.

During the days of steam, the Southern's motive power was a railfan/photographer's wonderland with the clean Ms-4's and the beautiful green and gold colored Ps-4 heavy Pacifics and the T-class Mountains-all providing the power for some of the most beautiful trains to ever keep the rails shiny.

*Credit: Photographer, David W. Salter; Curt Tillotson Collection.*

No. 6327 (Ms-4 class heavy 2-8-2): drivers, 63"; engine weight, 326,000 lbs.; steam pressure, 200 lbs.; tractive effort, 59,600 lbs.; superheated; Richmond built, 1926; tender weight (loaded with 10,000 gal. of water and 16 tons of coal); 191,400 lbs.; engine & tender length, 83' 1/16"; engine height, 14'11"; Elesco feedwater heater; Standard stoker; Hodges trailer trucks; retired, Jan. of 1953 (scrapped at Ferguson, Ky.).

With the semaphore signal indicating "clear track" ahead, this first section of No. 59 "pours it on" in a scene guaranteed to put a smile on the face of every railfan as well as an excitement that would permeate throughout their (and my) entire body.

The first section of this southbound freight leans into an elevated curve as the engineer pulled his throttle far back on its quadrant while the fireman opened the stoker in order to keep enough steam in Southern's handsome and heavy 2-8-2, No. 6327, so that the big "Mike" would respond to the "hogger's" demands. Looking at this outstanding photo, one could conclude (correctly) that the Mikado was doing just that: moving tonnage at a fast pace near Stearns, Ky. (192 miles south of Cincinnati) on the Southern's CNO&TP this cold afternoon in Nov. of 1946 (notice that old style "cattle car" hooked on No. 6327's tender).

It had that long Wimble smoke deflector attached to the top of the 2-8-2's steam and sand domes. Back in 1946 the practice of assigning engines to certain districts was still in effect. And with that smoke duct on No. 6327, you know that the big "Mike", which arrived on the Southern from the Richmond (Alco) plant in 1926, had traveled thousands of miles up and down this important segment of the road for over 20 years. This practice would continue until 1948-1949, when the Southern had enough diesels available to place both freight and passenger steam locomotives into a power "pool." As a result, it became a rare sight to seen an engine assigned to a certain area, actually still working in that area. Both the Ms-4'a and Ps-4's could be found on any of the Southern's main lines during the waning days of steam operations.

Just look at this burly, but esthetically pleasing, Elesco feedwater heater-equipped Ms-4. It's loaded with numerous appliances-all designed to improve its efficiency-and yet, everything about this "fire-breathing," steam and steel "monster" looked so right, so well balanced. And, with this active "volcano" spewing out that magnificent volume of smoke, railroading just does not get much better than this!

*Credit: Photographer, Doyle Inman; Curt Tillotson Collection.*

World War II, there was an army soldier stationed in this structure to help prevent any possible sabotage to this vital bridge.

A big, handsome, Elesco feedwater heater equipped Southern Ms-4 heavy Mikado, No. 4899, was really "balling the jack" with a long line of loaded refrigerator cars, running as 1st No. 251, between Atlanta and Birmingham. Notice the fine flow of smoke trailing back, close to the top of its cars-an indication that No. 4899 was pushing the maximum speed limit allowed on this section of the mainline-while the fireman gave a friendly "wave" to the photographer.

Coming straight at you was 326,000 lbs. of locomotive with white colored driver rims, walkways, and a big steamboat whistle, leaning forward in order to give a maximum sound when the engineer pulled the whistle cord in order to warn anyone and everyone to "get out of the way for I'm coming through!"

No. 4899 (Ms-4 class heavy 2-8-2): drivers, 63"; engine weight, 326,000 lbs.; steam pressure, 200 lbs.; tractive effort, 59,600 lbs.; superheated; Baldwin built, 1928; tender weight (loaded with 10,000 gal. of water and 16 tons of coal); 191,400 lbs.; engine & tender length, 83' 1/16"; engine height, 14'11"; Elesco feedwater heater; Standard stoker; Hodges trailer trucks; retired, April of 1952 (sold to the Baltimore Steel Co.).

You wanted to witness steam power in action? If so, take a good, long look at this thrilling photo taken on a cloudy, warm afternoon this Sept. 25th day in 1946, near Chattahoochee, Ga., as this mass of steam and steel rush at you between 50-55 m.p.h. and nearing the photogenic bridge over the Chattahoochee River. Speaking of the bridge, notice that "shack" on the left. During

The rushing sounds of a long freight approaching your location at high speed cannot be adequately put into words. You had to experience the event to know what it was like. The Ms-4's could not only lug the tonnage of a freight train, they also had the capacity to do the job at great speed. First No. 251 was a prime example of the abilities of these popular 2-8-2's to do it all!

This was how exciting railroading was when steam kept the rails shiny. I cannot think of any other example of steam, steel and speed than what we see here in this outstanding moment frozen for all time on film.

*Credit: Photographer, Unknown; Curt Tillotson Collection.*

No. 6625 (Ms-4 class heavy 2-8-2) and No. 6619 (Ms-1 class light 2-8-2): drivers, 63" (both); engine weight: No. 6625, 326,000 lbs.; No. 6619, 292,000 lbs.; steam pressure, 200 lbs. (both); tractive effort: No. 6625, 59,600 lbs.; No. 6619, 54,600 lbs.; tender weight: No. 6625 (loaded with 10,000 gal. of water and 16 tons of coal), 191,400 lbs.; No. 6619 (loaded with 10,000 gal. of water and

No. 4869 (Ms-4 class heavy 2-8-2): drivers, 63"; engine weight, 326,000 lbs.; steam pressure, 200 lbs.; tractive effort, 59,600 lbs.; superheated; Richmond built, 1926; tender weight (loaded with 10,000 gal. of water and 16 tons of coal); 191,400 lbs.; engine & tender length, 83' 1/16"; engine height, 14'11"; Elesco feedwater heater; Standard stoker; Hodges trailer trucks; retired, April of 1952 (sold to the Baltimore Steel Co.).

A heavy, shiny-railed double track main line, along with a gentle elevated curve and a short-but impressive-bridge, with an abundance of fall foliage in the background. These are all the ingredients necessary to have a railfan/photographer spend some time in order to record this bucolic setting. However, one last touch is needed to make his exposure perfect: a steam powered locomotive, heading north with a long train at speed.

The area described was found on the Southern's main line between Atlanta and Austell, Ga.-near Mabeton, Ga.-crossing over the Nickjack Creek Bridge on Nov. 16, 1947. And the "last touch" needed had just appeared: 2nd No. 54, powered by an impressive Ms-4 class 2-8-2, No. 4869, making good time plus producing an excellent smoke effect as well. Now, with all the items in place, the photographer could make his exposure, capturing on film the Southern's standard main line freight engine in action.

Austell (located approximately 18 miles north of Atlanta) was a great place to be, especially during the days of steam operation, for here the Southern's main line split. Heading north out of Austell would get a train to Chattanooga, while heading west you could travel to Birmingham. As a result, with all the action funneling into the area heading to or coming from Atlanta made for a great number of trains which would increase your chances to photograph a large number of train action shots.

The vast majority of freights were powered by the heavy Mikados while passenger runs usually had the beautiful, green and gold colored, renowned Ps-4 heavy Pacifics up front.

Yes, looking at this outstanding photo, I would say that our photographer picked an excellent place to record this thrilling flow of north and southbound movements with most of the trains being powered by "steam and steel!"

*Credit: Photographer, R. D. Sharpless; Curt Tillotson Collection.*

14 tons of coal), 183,200 lbs.; Richmond built: 1926 (No. 6625) and 1922 (No. 6619); engine & tender length: No. 6625, 83' 1/16"; and No. 6619, 81'5 1/2"; engine height, 14'11" (both); Elesco feedwater heater (No. 6625 only); Hodges trailer trucks (both); Standard stoker (both); retired: No. 6625 (May of 1953, finally scrapped at Finley, Alabama); No. 6619 (Oct. of 1957, sold to the Baltimore Steel Co.).

When you discovered that an approaching train had double-headed motive power, one of the first things that would come to mind could be: two steam locomotives, slugging it out at 15-20 m.p.h., using all their tractive effort to keep its tonnage moving. However, your first impression might not always be correct.

Another fascination about being near a main line is demonstrated in this exciting and surprising photo. Instead of two engines struggling at low speed to move its train, this extra west's steam engines were traveling at 50+ m.p.h.-to the pleasant surprise of the photographer.

The place was Helfin, Alabama on Dec. 6, 1947, a cold but beautiful morning, with this Birmingham-bound freight traveling the Southern's Washington-New Orleans main line. Helfin was 720.9 miles from our nation's capital, 83.4 miles from Atlanta and 82.4 miles from the extra west's destination: the "Pittsburgh of the South."

Here was an excellent opportunity to compare a Southern's heavy 2-8-2, in this case No. 6625, with a light Ms-1 class Mikado, No. 6619-both teaming up to move 87 cars of freight west to Birmingham-IN A HURRY!

With 87 cars in tow, it was too much tonnage for a lone Ms-1 to handle since, even though it would be on "big rails," there were a few short but sharp grades between Atlanta and Birmingham. As a result, the "boys" at Atlanta's roundhouse assigned the big Ms-4 to help out. Both engines were originally assigned to the Southern's AGS (Alabama Great Southern) district when they arrived from Richmond. Within less than three years, these engine assignments would end with the increasing number of diesels moving more and more trains. As a result, locomotives such as Nos. 6625 and 6619 went into a freight power pool, which meant they could be found almost anywhere they were needed on the Southern. The remainder of their years of service was spent in this fashion.

On this particular day, however, both engines were clean and traveling the main line in all their glory, doing what they were designed to do, in a style that only could be produced by the steam locomotive-awesome!

*Credit: Photographer, R. D. Sharpless; Curt Tillotson Collection.*

No. 4868 (Ms-4 class heavy 2-8-2): drivers, 63"; engine weight, 326,000 lbs.; steam pressure, 200 lbs.; tractive effort, 59,600 lbs.; superheated; Richmond built, 1926; tender weight (loaded with 10,000 gal. of water and 16 tons of coal); 191,400 lbs.; engine & tender length, 83' 1/16"; engine height, 14'11"; Elesco feedwater heater; Standard stoker; Hodges trailer trucks; retired, Oct. of 1952 (sold to the Baltimore Steel Co.).

The Southern's Washington-Atlanta, double track main line was a wondrous place to be during the days of steam operations. Since my dad's hometown was Greer, S. C.-approximately 13 miles from Greenville, S. C. (headquarters for the Charlotte Division)-I can remember the Ms-4's blasting through town with the engineer blowing that big, beautiful-sounding whistle for the three major crossings in town. And those green and gold-colored Ps-4's were breathtakingly magnificent. In fact, the Ps-4 powered trains that did not stop in Greer, came through at such a great speed that the "hogger" only blew the "two long-one short-one long" crossing whistle signal just once, with the melodious and hauntingly wonderful sounding steamboat whistle. The renowned heavy Pacific was making such good time that the varnish had passed all three crossings when the engineer completed the crossing signal routine. Indeed, the Ps-4's stack talk reminded me of a machine gun firing a long burst. There were over 50 trains per day at this time.

This Extra 4868 South was put together in Greenville and, after a few hours of traveling, the extra was in the Norcross, Ga. this early morning on Aug. 2, 1947, with only 15 minutes remaining before entering Atlanta, Ga. with the Inman Yard being its destination.

The graphite on No. 4868's smokebox was still fresh and the overall appearance of the 2-8-2 was still clean, even after the 153-mile journey down from Greenville. This was the Southern's way of keeping their motive power not only impressive in the "looks" department, but in excellent operational condition as well.

As you can see, this extra had quite a long train. I imagine the Greenville yardmaster cleared out several of his tracks when the extra headed south in the dark of night. No. 4868's extra tonnage caused its fireman to use his stoker far more often than usual to keep the proper amount of steam in this admired class of 2-8-2's. Indeed, many railfans feel that the Elesco feedwater heater equipped Ms-4's were second only to the Elesco feedwater equipped, green and gold colored Ps-4 heavy Pacific, in esthetically pleasing appearance. This was my feeling as well. Just look at this most impressive 2-8-2, heading down the historic main line of the Southern with over 70 cars in tow. Now, can you truthfully say we were all wrong in our opinion?

*Credit: Photographer, R. D. Sharpless; Curt Tillotson Collection.*

No. 4901 (Ms-4 class heavy 2-8-2): drivers, 63"; engine weight, 326,000 lbs.; steam pressure, 200 lbs.; tractive effort, 59,600 lbs.; superheated; Baldwin built, 1928; tender weight (loaded with 10,000 gal. of water and 16 tons of coal); 191,400 lbs.; engine & tender length, 83' 1/16"; engine height, 14'11"; Elesco feedwater heater; Standard stoker; Hodges trailer trucks; retired, Nov. of 1952.

White flags indicate that this big, handsome Southern Ms-4 class heavy Mikado, No. 4901, had an extra freight in tow, heading north, approximately 10 miles out of Atlanta (since it was only 10 miles north of "Big A" could help explain why the white flags were still so white), traveling towards Greenville, S. C. and points north on the road's Charlotte Division district of the Washington-Atlanta, double track, automatic block protected main line, this beautiful morning on Sept. 3, 1946. What a way to start a railfan's day!

No. 4901 was among the last batch of steam locomotives purchased by the Southern. Baldwin built No. 4885 through No. 4914 in 1928. This batch of 2-8-2's were used extensively over the Southern's main lines, especially the Washington-Atlanta, Atlanta to Chattanooga, Atlanta-Macon runs as well as the Greensboro to Selma, N. C. route and from Selma to Pinners Point, Va. over the trackage of the ACL. In the dying days of steam operations, you could occasionally find an Ms-4 heading up a freight between Charlotte, N. C. and Columbia, S. C. as well as part of the road's Birmingham Division.

The engineer had on a white shirt (!) and was gradually pulling back the throttle of his "steed" while his fireman opened his stoker-all in order to get this extra north up to main line speed (usually 50-55 m.p.h. or possibly faster). This impressive curve helped to accentuate the handsome lines of the clean 2-8-2 and to observe the rolling stock in this extra's consist.

How would it have been if we could have been in the cab of No. 4901 from Atlanta to Greenville, watching the crew at work, observing the southbound trains passing by, going "into the hole" for a faster northbounder to go by-probably a Ps-4 powered passenger train? What a memorable and spectacular adventure that would have been-Wow!

*Credit: Photographer, R. D. Sharpless; Curt Tillotson Collection.*

No. 4866 (Ms-4 class heavy 2-8-2): driver, 63"; engine weight, 326,000 lbs.; steam pressure, 200 lbs.; tractive effort, 59,600 lbs.; superheated; Richmond built, 1926; tender weight (loaded with 10,000 gal. of water and 16 tons of coal); 191,400 lbs.; engine & tender length, 83' 1/16"; engine height, 14'11"; Elesco feedwater heater; Standard stoker; Hodges trailer trucks; retired, Oct. of 1952 (sold to the Baltimore Steel Co.).

As our country began to recover from the effects of the Great Depression, business started to increase for the Southern and other roads. The Southern's reputation for engine care was also seen on a more frequent basis. A good example of this exemplary affection for "their" locomotives was shown in this photo.

Train No. 156 is shown departing Atlanta, Ga. for a run up to Greenville, S. C. and points north on the road's Washington-Atlanta double track, automatic block protected main line. The roundhouse crews in Atlanta made sure that the motive power assigned for this "hot" through freight, Ms-4 class heavy 2-8-2, No. 4866, got a fresh coating of graphite on its smoke box (because this part of the engine was too hot for ordinary paint, they used graphite) and fresh white paint was placed on the running boards, pony trucks and the entire engine was washed-just look how clean they got that beautiful and efficient Elesco feedwater heater (located in front of No. 4866's equally clean smokestack). However, for some reason they did not place white paint on the 2-8-2's driver rims which was a common practice. Possibly, after No. 4866 was assigned to a main line run, the crews did not have time to put this usual touch for "their" engine. Still, No. 156's train had a handsome Ms-4 on the point of this long freight heading north on this early morning (approximately 11:00 a.m.) in Sept. of 1936. Ahead was a 153-mile "adventure" for both of No. 4866's crew as well as the people who had the opportunity to see this heavy Mikado in action and hear that steamboat whistle which had such a wonderful and memorable sound.

Atlanta was a "beehive" of rail activity by 1936 with several major roads serving the rapidly growing city. And passenger business was so brisk that you could travel to almost any point of our country. Today, however, there are only two varnishes serving this major city: the north and southbound Amtrak's "Crescent"-running between New York and New Orleans. Freight business is excellent; however, it is still hard to believe that a city of this size only has these two streamliners for passenger service.

*Credit: Photographer, Collection of Harold K. Vollrath; Curt Tillotson Collection.*

No. 4869 (Ms-4 class heavy 2-8-2): driver, 63"; engine weight, 326,000 lbs.; steam pressure, 200 lbs.; tractive effort, 59,600 lbs.; superheated; Richmond built, 1926; tender weight (loaded with 10,000 gal. of water and 16 tons of coal); 191,400 lbs.; engine & tender length, 83' 1/16"; engine height, 14'11"; Elesco feedwater heater; Standard stoker; Hodges trailer trucks; retired, April of 1952 (sold to the Baltimore Steel Co.).-FTA (#4125) plus a "B" and another "A" unit.

"The Meet:" the "shotgunner" and the "growler:" the past and the future!

At least for a few years, these two forms of motive power operated together, helping the Southern become one of the most admired, progressive and successful railroads in the country.

The Southern realized-as far back as 1939-that the diesel-electric was not only the wave of the future for railroad motive power but also the savior of American railroads in general.

If it had not been for the tremendous demands of World War II, both in manpower and material, the Southern would have been completely dieselized before the end of the 1940s. But after 1945, when diesel motive power became more available, the big change began; between 1945 and 1953, you could find the road's exceptional fleet of steam power, albeit rather old (the last new steam locomotive purchased by the Southern was in 1928), still in good operational condition (in general), being rapidly replaced by the diesels.

This photo was taken in Jan. of 1950 and steam powered trains were becoming rare. Train No. 160, powered by Ms-4 class No. 4869, is shown "in the hole" near Dallas, Ga., while a long, southbound extra-led by F-TA model diesel, with No. 4125 in the lead of this A-B-A power consist-on its way to Atlanta (38 miles to the south) while steam powered No. 160 was heading to Chattanooga.

No. 4869's engineer and fireman can be seen in the 2-8-2's cab window while the head end brakeman came out of the "dog house," located on top of the tender-all to inspect the extra's train as well as to have a good look at the three "oil burners." The conductor and rear end brakeman of the extra south would inspect No. 160's train as they passed by.

This was a rare meet to say the least but it gave us an opportunity to see what it was like having the glorious past, represented by the impressive No. 4869, meet and, for a while, work with the future, whose representative was the lead F-TA on the extra south.

It was an excellent exposure, capturing the past and the future railroad motive power working together. I must admit, even though I know it's wrong, it is most tempting to remain in the past when railroading was far more exciting, especially when it came to motive power!

*Photographer, Unknown; Curt Tillotson Collection.*

No. 4896 (Ms-4 class heavy 2-8-2): drivers, 63"; engine weight, 326,000 lbs.; steam pressure, 200 lbs.; tractive effort, 59,600 lbs.; superheated; Baldwin built, 1928; tender weight (loaded with 10,000 gal. of water and 16 tons of coal); 191,400 lbs.; engine & tender length, 83' 1/16"; engine height, 14'11"; Elesco feedwater heater; Standard stoker; Hodges trailer trucks; retired; Oct. of 1952 (sold to the Baltimore Steel Co.).

There was very little information included with this photo except: it was made in Dec. of 1945 and it was a northbound freight leaving Atlanta, Ga. in the afternoon.

Even though there were few details accompanying this exposure, several clues could be used in helping us in gathering additional material on this photo. First, with the sun on the right of the train, this would support the supposition that the photo was made between 1:00 and 4:00 p.m. this Dec. day in '45. At this time of day, Southern's No. 156 would be heading north towards Greenville, S. C. on the road's Charlotte Division-part of the busy Washington-Atlanta main line. Secondly, Ms-4, No. 4896-the usual motive power for main line freights at this time-had the train moving at a good "clip," with a strong west-to-east wind whipping the big 2-8-2's smoke to the side. And thirdly, this was obviously a double track, automatic block protected main line and the track on the right (the southbound main) would soon be receiving new rails.

There was one other clue; however, it is unexplainable to me. The signal on the right had "260.9" on its poll. Numbers on a signal were usually a milepost indication. The Atlanta area was near mileposts 633 to 637.8 (Inman Yard). As a result, this was the only remaining piece of the puzzle I cannot explain.

Still, we know that the clean, Elesco feedwater heater equipped Ms-4 class No. 4896-with that large, prominent steamboat whistle (seen on it's top)-was making good time with this long freight on a cold, windy but sunny afternoon, It provided us with another opportunity to view the main line when the popular Ms-4 heavy Mikados were the standard main line freight motive power while the elegant Ps-4 heavy 4-6-2's provided power for practically all passenger trains. As Archie Bunker would say: "Those were the days." I agree with his statement 100%!.

*Credit: Photographer, Unknown; Curt Tillotson Collection.*

If one Southern Ms-4 heavy Mikado pulling a through freight at speed was exciting, what about two of these handsome 2-8-2's pulling this fast freight together? That's precisely what we have here: No. 4905 and No. 4909 heading an extra westbound freight just out of Atlanta's Inman Yard on its way towards Birmingham, 165 miles away, at 40 m.p.h.-and climbing-this beautiful morning on March 13, 1947. Now, this was railroading at its best, Southern style, during the days of steam operation!

Both engines were among the last new steam locomotives purchased by the Southern-from Baldwin in 1928-and the Ms-4 became the standard main line freight motive power on the road (and they remained so for over 20 years), since they met all the parameters established by the Southern for an effective and efficient freight mover. Indeed, the combination of Ms-4's and the elegant green and gold colored Ps-4's held down the train assignments (both freight and passenger) on the main lines of the road until the arrival of that "pesky thing" called a diesel-electric locomotive.

The yardmaster at Inman Yard needed to clear up a few tracks, so this extra west had more cars and tonnage that was usually assigned to an Ms-4. As a result, the roundhouse crew had a clean 2-8-2, No. 4905, available; and, because of this situation, we had a doubleheader heading to the "Pittsburgh of the South," in order to not just get the train there, but to get it to its destination ASAP! With two Ms-4's on the same freight, I feel confident that this magnificent combination of power did just that.

Next to the Ps-4 heavy Pacifics, the Elesco feedwater heater equipped Ms-4's were the most revered steam locomotives both among the railfans and the Southern employees as well. Looking at this scene, I feel we can understand why this was so. Wouldn't you agree?

*Credit: Photographer, David W. Salter; Curt Tillotson Collection.*

No. 4871 (Ms-4 class heavy 2-8-2): drivers, 63"; engine weight, 326,000 lbs.; steam pressure, 200 lbs.; tractive effort, 59,600 lbs.; superheated; Richmond built, 1926; tender weight (loaded with 10,000 gal. of water and 16 tons of coal); 191,400 lbs.; engine & tender length, 83' 1/16"; engine height, 14'11"; Elesco feedwater heater; Standard stoker; Hodges trailer trucks; retired, April of 1952 (sold to the Baltimore Steel Co.).

During the steam era, the Southern, like many other roads, ran far more extra movements as compared to today's diesel operations. There were several reasons why this practice was followed. A Southern Ms-4 class heavy 2-8-2 could handle between 50-80 cars in a train if the tonnage was not too great. Doubleheading was not that uncommon to avoid this dramatic procedure since a doubleheader meant two crews on one train. This was costly and it tied up the additional crew. On the other hand, the diesel could pull almost as much tonnage as a yardmaster could tie onto the engine's rear coupler. If there was too much tonnage, you simply added another unit and another, if necessary. Regardless of how many units were needed, you still had only one crew. During the steam period, if you had a fruit extra (peaches, apples, watermelon, etc.) with-say-50 cars, the Southern would send the perishable on its way as an extra movement. With the diesel, however, the road would wait for maximum tonnage before moving the produce.

A case in point is shown here with an extra west, powered by a mostly clean, graphite covered smokebox Ms-4, No. 4871, with an Elesco feedwater heater and steamboat whistle equipped heavy 2-8-2, really rolling at a good 50 m.p.h. this cold but beautiful afternoon in Dec. of 1948, near Villa Rica, Ga. with 62 cars, on its way from Atlanta to Birmingham. It was 37 miles from Atlanta with 129 more miles to go before reaching its destination on this excellent section of automatic block protected double track and all with a clear stack (watch out for an extra amount of hot cinders).

The frequent and shot train practice was followed more closely during the steam era. The 200+ car trains were found during the diesel period. However, even with the diesel's prowess, some roads went back to the idea of more frequent and shorter movements since it gave the customers better service, not to mention that it helped to eliminate numerous broken couplers and other problems that came with enormous pressures placed on equipment in a 200 car, 2+ mile long train.

An Ms-4, with clean white flags, running down the big rails of a main line with driver rods a blur was an exciting drama; and, even with steam power, the frequent-shorter train idea it did offer the shippers better service plus the fact that you had more trains to photograph, was a railfan's delight when steam controlled the freight and passenger assignments. What a wonderful experience!

*Credit: Photographer, Unknown; Curt Tillotson Collection.*

No 4823 (Ms-4 class heavy 2-8-2): drivers, 63"; engine weight, 326,000 lbs.; steam pressure, 200 lbs.; tractive effort, 59,600 lbs.; superheated; Richmond built, 1923; tender weight (loaded with 10,000 gal. of water and 16 tons of coal); 191,400 lbs.; engine & tender length, 83' 1/16"; engine height, 14'11"; Worthington feedwater heater; Standard stokers; Hodges trailer trucks; retired, April of 1952 (sold to the Baltimore Steel Co.).

A big Southern Ms-4 class Mikado, making a good 50+ m.p.h., with green flags flapping and driving rods flailing, take to the air as it crossed a long, tall bridge-now this was rail action at its best: both thrilling and scary, all at the same time!

During the steam era, most bridges, even many that carried the tremendous tonnage of main line traffic, were made of some wood and a majority of steel. As a result, to prevent major damage to the structure due to fire, the Southern had several platforms built on the edge of the bridges. A 50 gal. drum filled with water was placed on each platform that could be used to combat any fire that might occur (you'll notice several of these extensions in this photo). These platforms were also used by anyone who might be walking on the bridge as a train was approaching so they could get out of the way of the roaring steam powered train.

Our "courageous" photographer took a position on one of these platforms in order to make this excellent exposure. Can you imagine being this close to a 326,000 lbs. Ms-4 approaching you at nearly a mile-a-minute pace with a thin volume of smoke curving back over its cars? The fast moving steel and steam "monster" growing larger and larger in your camera's viewfinder; and, with all his fright, he remembered to release his shutter. As a result of his risking life and limb, we are able to see what it was like to have this magnificent engine with several tons of freight coming straight at you and passing just a few feet from your body. It was a foolish move on his part but I can understand why he did it. He wanted to get an action and dramatic feel of steam at its best. He surely accomplished his goal!

First No. 253 was headed by Ms-4 class heavy 2-8-2, No. 4823, pulling 47 cars as it crossed over the Chattahoochee (Ga.) River Bridge on Aug. 25, 1946 this late, hot and humid afternoon, bound for Birmingham with a vengeance!

The bridge was trembling with nearly a million tons of locomotive and train approaching the photographer at 55+ m.p.h. mark. To say it was an awesome moment would be an understatement. I must admit that I did the same thing on a few occasions when I was much younger and felt immortal. Apparently, youth tends to put personal safety aside and nothing would stop you from fulfilling your goal of recording such action as this. I imagine the engineer, who was looking at this "crazy" person, and the photographer both held their breath and crossed their fingers and hoped nothing would happen. Obviously, nothing happened except an outstanding photo was made, one that we can all admire in the comfort and safety of our home. Well done , Mr. Sharpless!

*Credit: Photographer, R. D. Sharpless; Curt Tillotson Collection.*

No. 4827 (Ms-4 class heavy 2-8-2): drivers, 63"; engine weight, 326,000 lbs.; steam pressure, 200 lbs.; tractive effort, 59,600 lbs.; superheated; Richmond built, 1923; tender weight (loaded with 10,000 gal. of water and 16 tons of coal); 191,400 lbs.; engine & tender length, 83' 1/16"; engine height, 14'11"; Worthington feedwater heater; Standard stoker; Hodges trailer trucks; retired, Aug. of 1954 (sold to David J. Joseph).

This photo helps to explain why the Southern selected the Ms-4 class heavy 2-8-2 as their standard main line freight mover. This class of "Mike" could lug tonnage upgrade-as shown (notice the difference between the rail colors)-and, out on the "big rails," i.e., the main line, it could also move the "hot shot" freights at an impressive pace. Not only did the Southern stick with the Ms-4s when other roads were purchasing newer, more powerful steam motive power with new wheel arrangements such as the 2-8-4's, 4-8-4's and even massive articulates, the 2-8-2's remained in service for an additional 5 years after the date of this photo.

There was another reason why the Southern kept their heavy Mikados on the main line, working freight assignments. The road decided back in 1940 they were going to dieselize their entire motive power roster. The Southern was so impressed with General Motive's Electro Motor Division (EMD's) A-B-B-A set of FT model diesels, which barnstormed from the east coast to the west in 1939-1940, that rather than invest huge sums of funds in newer steam power, the astute Southern knew the diesel was the wave of the future for American railroads. Only the incredible needs of World War II delayed the road from dieselizing their power at an earlier date (a goal finally achieved on June 17, 1953).

This extra is shown using all of its 59,600 lbs. of tractive effort, with its stoker wide opened while the engineer was watching the drivers of his steed, No. 4827 (as well as the photographer) leaving Birmingham, passing through Gate City, Ala., heading for Chattanooga-143 miles away-this March 21, 1948-all in the dramatic, thunderous style that only a steam locomotive could produce.

The sounds of this heavy 2-8-2 working at full throttle, the ground trembling, the aroma of coal smoke, steam and hot grease was a pleasurable smell to a railfan. However, efficiency would win over nostalgia every time-as it should. Still, such action as displayed here was a special occurrence. Indeed, it was an event that once seen would never be forgotten. As a result, the efficiency of the diesel-electric won the day; but, in our memory (which was reinforced by such moments depicted here) would always be in our hearts and in our soul!

*Credit: Photographer, Frank E. Ardrey, Jr.; Curt Tillotson Collection.*

No. 4802 (Ms-4 class heavy 2-8-2): drivers, 63"; engine weight, 326,000 lbs.; steam pressure, 200 lbs.; tractive effort, 59,600 lbs.; superheated; Richmond built, 1923; tender weight (loaded with 10,000 gal. of water and 16 tons of coal); 191,400 lbs.; engine & tender length, 83' 1/16"; engine height, 14'11"; Worthington feed-water heater; Standard stoker; Hodges trailer trucks; retired, Aug. 22, 1952 (scrapped at Haynes-Spartanburg, S. C.).

Coming out of Atlanta and passing through Austell, Ga., Extra 4802 North is shown leaving double track territory and entering the automatic block protected, single track main line on its way to Chattanooga with 67 cars in tow.

Southern's Ms-4, No. 4802, is shown gathering speed as it crosses over the Sweetwater Creek Bridge this beautiful March 19, 1948. As usual, before leaving Atlanta, the roundhouse crews made sure this 2-8-2 was presentable: its smoke box had a fresh coating of graphite, its walkways had white paint applied and its driver rims were also given the white paint treatment as well. Now, the Southern's reputation for having the most handsome engines in the rail industry was maintained.

What a magnificent scene: a big, handsome, heavy Mikado, hauling over half-a-mile of freight cars on a "hot" main line, crossing over a most photogenic bridge with a semaphore signal in the background. And the big "girl's" fireman had just shut off his stoker as the extra north began to make good time. Another "adventure" was about to begin for No. 4802's crew as it headed towards Chattanooga. All these ingredients made for a railfan's delight, plus it brought more funds for the Southern's coffers.

Looking at the debris gathered at the bottom of the bridge supports, there must have been a recent rain storm that passed through the area. Today, the bridge is a solid steel structure and the traffic through the area is controlled by C.T.C. with a modern signal replacing the old reliable semaphore blades.

It must have been thrilling for the photographer to find such action at this beautiful location. Thankfully, he recorded his excitement on film so that we can share his enthusiasm when he froze, for all time, steam power-not in excursion service-but doing what it was designed to do (and doing it quite well, I might add).

*Credit: Photographer, Unknown; Curt Tillotson Collection.*

No. 4822 and No 4804 (Ms-4 class heavy 2-8-2s): drivers, 63" (both); engine weight, 326,000 lbs. (both); steam pressure, 200 lbs. (both); tractive effort, 59,600 lbs. (both); Richmond built, 1923 (both); tender weight (loaded with 10,000 gal. of water and 16 tons of coal); 191,400 lbs. (both); engine & tender length, 83' 1/16" (both); engine height, 14'11" (both); Worthington feedwater heater (both); Standard stoker (both); Hodges trailer trucks (both); retired, No. 4822 (March of 1952) and No. 4804 (Nov. of 1952-sold to the Baltimore Steel Co.).

Two powerful Southern Ms-4 heavy 2-8-2s, No. 4822 and No. 4804, team up to pull this first section of a northbound, extra long and heavy, through freight out of Atlanta, Ga. on its way to Chattanooga-148 miles away-on a beautiful afternoon this April 19, 1947.

The two "Mikes" had just cleared Atlanta's Inman Yard-just beyond the deep cut in the background-and began to get its tonnage moving at a good pace. The roundhouse crews did their job of making the two Ms-4s "presentable" as they headed north. There was graphite covering their smoke boxes and just look at the unbelievably clean cab and tender of No. 4822! Wow, if you did not know better, you would believe they were new. Even the massive Worthington feedwater heater hung just above the driver's No. 3 and 4, was immaculate. The smoke stacks also had the impressive graphite covering.

What a beautiful location to make this exposure. And, to have two Ms-4s, doubleheading, passing by, was just "icing on the cake." Today, however, this bucolic setting no longer exists. This entire area was swallowed up when Inman Yard was doubled in size and became a modern "push button" type facility that could handle thousands of cars per day in a far more efficient manner. Progress does take a toll on the past.

As a result, today's SD-70s, D9-40CWs, and other similar diesel "monsters" carry the tonnage out of Inman and on to Chattanooga over big, continuous rail under C.T.C. and automatic block protection. Now, which would be more dramatic in these northbound movements: two or more six-axle diesels or two Ms-4s really digging in to get its train moving? To me, it would be no problem in deciding an answer to this question.

I wonder what No. 4822's fireman was shouting to his companion on No. 4804?

*Credit: Photographer, Unknown; Curt Tillotson Collection.*

of this double track line, roared a Southern Ms-4, heavy Mikado, No. 4804, with 76 cars in tow, making 50+ m.p.h. Now, this was a moment in rail history that deserved to be preserved. Thankfully, there was a railfan/photographer in the area this beautiful early morning and recorded on film No. 4804, with its stoker on and the smoke emerging from the graphite-covered smokestack, trailing off and along the top of its cars. This was a sure sign that the 2-8-2 was really "making time" on its way to Atlanta, Ga.'s Inman Yard, while the wonderful whistle continued to blow as the millions of pounds of locomotive and its consist was approaching a nearby highway crossing.

This was a scene and event designed to awaken the souls of not only railfans but even the ordinary "audience" who were fortunate enough to be able to see this thrilling drama unfolding before them.

No. 4804 (Ms-4 class heavy 2-8-2): drivers, 63"; engine weight, 326,000 lbs.; steam pressure, 200 lbs.; tractive effort, 59,600 lbs.; Richmond built, 1923; tender weight (loaded with 10,000 gal. of water and 16 tons of coal); 191,400 lbs.; engine & tender length, 83' 1/16"; engine height, 14'11"; Worthington feedwater heater; Standard stoker; Hodges trailer trucks; retired, Nov. of 1952 (sold to the Baltimore Steel Co.).

A noticeable "rumbling," then the sounds of a steamboat's melodious "warning" followed by staccato stack-talking growing louder and louder. All of a sudden from around an elevated curve

With that graphite-covered smoke box, walkways and parts of the "push polls" and upper portions of No. 4804's cowcatcher, this Ms-4-among the first batch of heavy 2-8-2s purchased by the Southern-really knew how to put on a show and yet, at the same time, fulfill its assignment with speed and efficiency: all indications of a Southern's regal looking steam locomotive at work.

Yes, this April morning in '48 was a fine time to photograph a road that lavished great care on its motive power and became known as a special and respected railroad among its peers.

*Credit: Photographer, Unknown; Curt Tillotson Collection.*

No. 6326 (Ms-4 class heavy 2-8-2): drivers, 63"; engine weight, 326,000 lbs.; steam pressure, 200 lbs.; tractive effort, 59,600 lbs.; Richmond built, 1926; tender weight (loaded with 10,000 gal. of water and 16 tons of coal); 191,400 lbs.; engine & tender length, 83' 1/16"; engine height, 14'11"; Elesco feedwater heater; Standard stoker; Hodges trailer trucks; retired, Aug. of 1954 (sold to David J. Joseph).

One look at this Southern Ms-4 class heavy 2-8-2 will help you understand why the railfans, as well as the connoisseurs of the steam locomotive, felt that the Ms-4s of the Southern were among the most attractive 2-8-2 freight motive power, not only on the Southern but, arguably, on any road, anywhere in our country.

Sitting on the big turntable in Chattanooga, this Dec. 19, 1935, No. 6326-a Mikado assigned to the road's CNO&TP-was being prepared for a trip back up the busy main line to Cincinnati. So far, the roundhouse crews had washed the 2-8-2, applied graphite to the smoke and fire boxes as well as No. 6326's smoke stack; white paint covered the walkways, driver and pony truck rims and it was thoroughly inspected. All that remained was for the hostler to take this handsome Ms-4 to the coal dock for more fuel and the water station where it would receive 10,000 gal. of future steam into its tender. And then No. 6326 would be moved to the ready track. Speaking of the 2-8-2's tender, the "Dog House"-a place for the head end brakeman to occupy on occasion-had its little windows washed and made shiny clear.

The Wimble duct (a smoke deflector located on the top of the engine's sand dome) automatically classed this efficient engine as being assigned to the rugged CNO&TP since during that 338-mile journey north, it would pass through that area known as the "Rat Hole." This nickname was appropriate since this segment included over 25 tunnels-some long, some short-deep, narrow cuts, sharp curves and about anything else the mountains could throw at the Southern's line. Approaching a tunnel, the engineer would activate the deflector which would then move forward, covering the smokestack and channel the smoke over (not into) the engine cab; the deflector also protected the tunnel's roofs from the blasting effects of the hard working engines.

Looking at this scene, I would rank the Elesco feedwater heater equipped Ms-4 just behind the magnificent and colorful Ps-4 heavy Pacific and the lean Ts-class Mountains when it comes to the "looks" department. Would you agree with my ranking?

No. 4870 (Ms-4 class heavy 2-8-2): drivers, 63"; engine weight, 326,000 lbs.; steam pressure, 200 lbs.; tractive effort, 59,600 lbs.; Richmond built, 1926; tender weight (loaded with 10,000 gal. of water and 16 tons of coal); 191,400 lbs.; engine & tender length, 83' 1/16"; engine height, 14'11"; Elesco feedwater heater; Standard stoker; Hodges trailer trucks; retired, April of 1952 (sold to the Baltimore Steel Co.).

Since we've had a good look at a Southern CNO&TP assigned Ms-4 class heavy 2-8-2 with its husky appearance, Elesco feedwater heater, Wimble smoke deflector and the other appliances necessary to help it through the "Rat Hole" section of the Chattanooga-Cincinnati run, we now have a view of an Ms-4 that was the main freight motive power on the Washington-Atlanta main line.

No. 4870 had just arrived at the Atlanta's Inman Yard's roundhouse area after an overnight freight run from Greenville, S. C. this early morning on Feb. 20, 1946. The regular crew had just departed the Charlotte Division based 2-8-2. Soon a hostler would take the big Ms-4 to the roundhouse where it would be inspected from "nose to tail." Then it would be washed to a sparkly clean shine, followed by a new coat of graphite to be added to both the smoke and fire boxes; its drivers and pony trucks would have their rims painted white along with walkways; the engine cab would be cleaned and its equipment polished. Finally, the hostler would get 10,000 gal. of water and 16 tons of coal placed into its tender; supplies for the new crew (fuses, rail torpedoes, flags, rags, ice water and cups, etc.) would be put on the engine cab and then this handsome locomotive would be placed on the ready track where it would be eventually assigned to move a northbound freight back to Greenville, possibly all the way to Spencer, N. C. This was the normal procedure followed once a steam locomotive had completed a run and was made ready for another trip over the main line.

This familiar routine was observed until the arrival of the diesel-electric motive power which did not require practically all of the care given to an Ms-4 to be made for a run. Soon, the roundhouse and many other crews would not be needed, nor coal or large quantities of water. As a result, thousands of employees found themselves jobless-many doing what their father's and their father's fathers had done for generations. The diesel, which required little maintenance, could travel the entire Washington-Atlanta main line without a change in motive power at Spencer. Indeed, the passenger train diesels could travel the entire distance between D. C. and New Orleans without any problems.

The appearance of the diesel was truly a revolution in the rail world. True, the diesels saved the railroads from bankruptcy and possible ruination. However, our memories were not and never will be affected by the "growlers." I remember steam in action and such photos appearing in this book will help others to remember the Golden Age of steam powered trains moving the nation's passengers and freight to their destinations.

*Credit: Photographer Unknown; Curt Tillotson Collection.*

No. 4844 (Ms-4 class heavy 2-8-2): drivers, 63"; engine weight, 326,000 lbs.; steam pressure, 200 lbs.; tractive effort, 59,600 lbs.; superheated; Schenectady built, 1924; tender weight (loaded with 10,000 gal. of water and 16 tons of coal); 191,400 lbs.; engine & tender length, 83' 1/16"; engine height, 14'11"; Worthington feedwater heater; Standard stoker; Hodges trailer trucks; retired, Aug. of 1954 (sold to David J. Joseph).

We have seen numerous, excellent photos depicting a Southern's Ms-4 heavy Mikado approaching a rail photographer in all the might and grandeur of this big, efficient and impressive steam locomotive, pulling tonnage in the famous steam and steel style that could only be described as both dramatic and memorable fashion. However, how did the huge 2-8-2's appear heading on its way after passing the railfan/photographer?

Engine No. 4844, heading the road's "hot" No. 153 southbound, passing by the Reidsville, N. C.'s passenger station (on the left) this late morning on Sept. 15, 1944, gives us a good view of the locomotive and its train traveling behind this lucky photographer, pulling with all its might in moving its freight consist towards its next stop-Greensboro, N. C.'s Pomona Yard-on the busy Washington-Atlanta main line: a most thrilling sight, to say the least! Indeed, "coming" or "going," the Southern's Ms-4 was a wondrous event to see and photograph.

The huge Worthington feedwater heater-hung over drivers #3 and #4-was most obvious; the big steamboat whistle was a prominent fixture near the steam dome (ahead of the fireman's cab). And the "Dog House" was seen on top of No. 4844's tender.

By 1944, World War II began winding down towards a glorious victory for the Allies; there was still a chance of sabotage of American transportation. Maybe that was why the fireman was looking at the photographer so closely. It was not easy picturing our railroads in action during the war years because of security reasons. We are truly fortunate that our "daring" cameraman was able to capture on film the mighty and beloved Ms-4 doing what it did the best; getting its train to its destination in the "Southern style" and, in this case, the 2-8-2 was heading south with a clear stack (darn it!).

*Credit: Photographer, David Driscoll; Curt Tillotson Collection.*

# The Powerful Sante Fe's, 2-10-2's

No. 5208: (Ss-1 class, 2-10-2's): drivers: 57"; engine weight: 352,000 lbs.; steam pressure: 200 lbs.; tractive effort: 69,400 lbs.; superheated; Cole trailer trucks; Brooks built: 1918; tender weight (loaded with 10,000 gal. of water and 16 tons of coal): 188,300 lbs.; engine & tender length: 86' 6 3/4"; engine height: 15'0"; retired: Dec. of 1949.

By the beginning of the 20th Century, the Southern and most all other railroads had major motive power problems to solve. Freight equipment was becoming heavier and the demands for locomotives to pull larger and longer trains at a faster pace, yet remain operationally economical, was great. Since the 2-8-0 Consolidation and older power could not perform within these parameters without constantly double-heading (a costly, albeit a great photographic opportunity), the Southern began to search for a solution to their dilemma.

More powerful and heavier locomotives were needed. In 1904, the first 2-10-2 wheel designed engines were made for the Santa Fe Railroad. Thus, the 2-10-2 wheel arrangement engines were forever known as Santa Fe's. The 2-10-2's raised some eyebrows among rail officials, including those of the Southern, since these huge locomotives proved to be quite successful. In fact, the Southern felt the 2-10-2 was the answer to their wishes. As a result, 25 of the 2-10-2's were ordered from Alco's Richmond plant in 1918; the Santa Fe's performed beyond the road's expectations. Eventually, the Southern had the largest fleet of 2-10-2's in the South.

One problem arose, however, because of the 2-10-2's long wheel base. How could they negotiate the numerous sharp curves found in the mountainous territory around the Asheville, N. C. and Knoxville, Tenn. areas? The answer: a Franklin lateral motion driving boxes device and a spherical bearing was applied to the forward connecting driving rods. All of these appurtenances were called "floating" front drivers. They all worked! Now the big "hogs" could be used on most Southern lines where their weight would not be a problem for bridges and light rails.

The new 2-10-2's actually went to work not only in the mountainous terrain but, during World War I, they could be found pulling tonnage on the Washington-Atlanta main line; they remained in service on this "hot" route until the arrival of the more versatile, faster and less costly Ms-4 2-8-2's. The Santa Fe's spent the remainder of their years mostly in the Asheville area, working the Saluda grade and Swannanoa Route as well as the Asheville-Knoxville line. They proved to be ideal motive power for working in the mountains. Only the diesel-electric engines could out-perform these beautiful "brutes."

Shown in this enlargement is No. 5208, an Ss-1 class 2-10-2, arriving in the Asheville yard with a solid coal train (running as a first section) on this hazy morning in Sept. of 1937. Because of their extra long wheel base, the Ss-1 could not operate on the Asheville-Salisbury or the Asheville-Spartanburg, S. C. lines, however.

Talk about big, the Ss-1's were simply huge and very powerful. Even with "drag" freights such as this coal extra, the Southern put graphite on No. 5208's smoke box, the engine jacket was clean, lettering and numbers were in gold paint; and with that huge steamboat whistle, they not only looked but sounded like extra big power-and the 2-10-2's were!

Since they had effective stokers, the fireman did not have to break his back keeping that massive firebox filled with coal. Notice the "rail washer" (below the fireman). It was used to wash off the rails after the heavy sanding needed to keep those 10 drivers from losing traction. No matter what angle you looked at the Southern 2-10-2's, they were huge and powerful engines. Only the Southern's even larger and more powerful 2-8-8-2's could out-perform these giants.

They were "ground shakers," photogenic, had a sharp and loud, cracking "stack talk." And, after they passed you, they created an image that was permanently placed in your mind!

*Photographer, Walt Thrall; Curt Tillotson Collection.*

Asheville area, passing the passenger station and mail & express facility (seen on the right).

This will be as far south as No. 5204 could go since its wheel base was longer than the Ss-class, 2-10-2's (which had "floating" devices placed on the first set of its drivers, enabling them to accommodate the sharp curves to Spartanburg, S. C. or east to Salisbury, N. C.). The Ss-1's worked between Asheville and Knoxville, as well as between Bristol and Chattanooga, Tenn.

The Ss-class was the most common 2-10-2's found in the "Land of the Sky." They not only provided head end power, but "pusher" assignments as well. It was rare if you did not find a passenger train heading up Saluda Grade with an Ss-class 2-10-2 "grunting" as hard as it could to conquer 4.7 to 5.01% of gravity. They were also found fore and aft of westbound freights leaving Old Fort, N. C., heading to Asheville as well.

After being coaled, watered, inspected and washed, No. 5204 would head back west to Knoxville and points north or south from there. It was difficult telling any major differences of the Ss from Ss-1's in the "looks" department. One thing they had in common, however; they were huge, powerful and right at home in the mountains.

*Photographer, Walt Thrall; Curt Tillotson Collection.*

No. 5204: (Ss-1 class, 2-10-2); drivers: 57"; engine weight: 352,000 lbs.; steam pressure: 200 lbs.; tractive effort, 69,400 lbs.: superheated; Cole trailer trucks; Brooks built: 1918; tender weight (loaded with 10,000 gal. of water and 16 tons of coal): 188,300 lbs.; engine & tender length: 86' 6 3/4"; engine height: 15'0"; retired: April of 1950.

The constant haze over Asheville, N. C. reminded me of the same condition that existed in Spencer, N. C. during the steam era-all caused by the great number of steam locomotives spewing the coal smoke out of their stacks.

This afternoon in Sept. of 1937, the haze was there as the first section of a freight from Knoxville, Tenn., pulled by a big and powerful Ss-1 class, 2-10-2-in this case it was No. 5204-arrived in the

No. 5021: (Ss-class, 2-10-2); drivers: 57"; engine weight: 370,000 lbs.; steam pressure: 200 lbs.; tractive effort: 73,600 lbs.; superheated; Cole trailer trucks; tender weight (loaded with 9,000 gal. of water and 12 tons of coal): 176,000 lbs.; engine & tender length: 84' 3 1/2"; engine height: 15'3"; retired: March of 1952.

Working up the incredible Saluda Grade is No. 5021, an Ss-class, 2-10-2, equipped with "floating" front drivers, pulling the first part of its Asheville, N. C. bound freight (with a fellow 2-10-2 on the rear, pushing at its full capacity) this August 3, 1948). Once in the town of Saluda, N. C., the two 2-10-2's will leave this cut of cars and then both Santa Fe's would drift back downgrade to Melrose, N. C.-the base of the grade-get the remainder of the freight and head back up the big climb. At 4.7%, it was the highest main line grade in the United States. Once it pulled into Saluda, the "helper" would head back to Melrose and wait to help the next Asheville bound freight or passenger train. Meanwhile, No. 5021 would re-assemble its train and then head on to the "Land of the Sky."

Notice, while on the 4.7% climb, the huge 2-10-2 appears to have a clear stack. This is a deception for the "stack-talk" was so loud that it bounced off the surrounding hills. I have discovered that when a steam locomotive was at full throttle, with little or no smoke coming out of its stack, be ready to be showered with a great amount of cinders-far more than when smoke was being exhausted.

This fireman was a "pro," for he had a clear stack, a small cloud of steam was emerging from the safety valve and the engineer had his throttle all the way back on its quadrant. The ground was shaking, the "stack talk" was so loud that it would rival a modern-day "boom box," and the joy of being a railfan was being reinforced with every turn of those 10 drivers. Man, it does not get any better than this!

*Photographer, August A. Thieme, Jr.; Curt Tillotson Collection.*

No. 5203: (Ss-1 class, 2-10-2): drivers, 57"; engine weight: 352,000 lbs.; steam pressure: 200 lbs.; tractive effort: 69,400 lbs.; superheated; Cole trailer trucks; Brooks built: 1918; tender weight (loaded with 10,000 gal. of water and 16 tons of coal): 188,300 lbs.; engine & tender length: 86' 6 3/4"; engine height: 15'0"; retired: Dec. of 1949.

Here we have an opportunity to see just how long 86' 6 3/4" truly was. The big and long Ss-1 class, 2-10-2 (No. 5203) is shown leaving Johnson City, Tenn. early on the morning of March 13, 1944 (9:30 a.m.) pulling a Knoxville, Tenn. bound freight — with great gusto!

The fireman on the huge, powerful and handsome "hog" had his stoker on to make sure the needle on his steam pressure gauge remained on the 200 lbs. level. No matter what locomotive it might be, Southern Railway engines always appeared clean, perfectly balanced in appearance — a sight to see and admire. No. 5203 was not an exception to these Southern traits. Even though this photo was made in 1944, the impressive 2-10-2 appeared on the road's roster in 1918! It would remain active until Dec. of 1949.

The Ss-1 class 2-10-2's could be found pulling great tonnage between Bristol, Knoxville and Chattanooga, Tenn. as well as moving freights to and from Asheville, N. C. However, they were not allowed south or east of Asheville since their very long wheel base would not do well on the numerous sharp curves encountered in those areas. The Southern equipped their Ss-class 2-10-2's with "floating" front drivers and this class of Santa Fe's dominated the line to Spartanburg, S. C. (down mighty Saluda Grade) and Salisbury, N. C. (the "Swannanoa Route"). So No. 5203 would visit Asheville on occasions. But the 2-10-2's and its sister Ss-1's held down the freight assignments in and around the Knoxville Division and those areas west of the Blue Ridge Mountains.

Can't you hear the loud "barking" of No. 5203 getting its train under way, shooting smoke and cinders skyward, creating a drama that could never be duplicated by the diesels.

*Photographer, Unknown; Curt Tillotson Collection.*

# The Massive 2-8-8-2's

The first Mallet type locomotive was built by Baldwin for the Great Northern in 1906. It had a 2-6-6-2 wheel arrangement and proved quite successful, especially in "pusher" service. As a result, the Southern's Alabama Great Southern segment of their system purchased the road's first compound "monster"-a 2-6-8-0 from Baldwin in 1906. Eventually, this first Mallet compound was transferred to the Southern's Asheville Division.

The Southern was so impressed with this Articulated's performance that they had Baldwin build them two 2-8-8-2's (Nos. 4002 and 4003) and classified them as "Ls" type engines. Then, during World War I, the road acquired No. 4004 through No. 4026 (from 1918 through 1926) and assigned them the classification as type "Ls-1's." They produced 84,350 lbs. of tractive effort-pulling power needed by the Southern. Then, in 1926, Baldwin sent the road what was to become the "Ls-2" class 2-8-8-2's (Nos. 4050 through 4058) which could muster 96,000 lbs. of tractive effort and thus became the biggest and most powerful steam locomotives ever owned by the Southern. These new "brutes" were sent to the Asheville and Appalachia divisions, moving coal trains and serving as "pushers" as well.

The Southern soon discovered that their Ls-2's performance would be enhanced if they were turned into a simple type of locomotive, i.e., both sets of cylinders would receive high pressure steam. No. 4050 was the first 2-8-8-2 to be converted from a compound to a simple Articulated. However, during the early 1930's, the Great Depression had caused business to decline to the point that the Southern could only afford to have Nos. 4018, 4021 and 4025 changed into simple 2-8-8-2's. Still, all the Ls-2's served the Southern well and were not removed from service until the arrival of the diesel-electrics.

Here we have "Mount Vesuvius on wheels!" Indeed, this huge and powerful Ls-2 class 2-8-8-2, No. 4056, is depicted passing through Weems, Alabama with a heavy and long Extra 4056 West freight train. The big Articulated was truly acting like a small Mt. Vesuvius, both in volume of smoke and sound-Wow! The fireman obviously has his stoker on and, with 96,000 lbs. of pulling power, there were no doubts that the 2-8-8-2 would get its tonnage to its destination.

Weems, Ala.-east of Birmingham, Ala.-was the place to be, especially this early morning in Feb. of 1946. You had the Southern's segment of the Atlanta-Birmingham portion of its Washington-New Orleans main line with Washington being 790 miles from this location (notice the mile post marker on the right). No. 4056 had just covered the Seaboard Air Line's trestle (their Atlanta-Birmingham line) in smoke and cinders and this area also felt the tonnage from both freight and passenger trains of the Central of Georgia as well. As a result, day or night, you had trains, trains, trains-a railfan's paradise! And there were numerous photogenic locations all around this area.

Just imagine what it would have been like being at Weems as this ponderous, most powerful and biggest steam locomotive every owned by the Southern, approached you-wide opened-with the "shotgunning" sounds producing decibels almost harmful to the human ear (but absolutely wonderful to railfans). The ground starts to shake, the main driving rods on the two sets of eight drivers, "clanking" so loud you expected them to fall off. And, after this magnificent drama passed by and things gradually returned to normal conditions-it would never be normal for you-for such action produced by No. 4056 would remain fresh in your mind for the remainder of your life.

Hopefully, the track crew on the "motor car"-on the left-would be able to enter the main line through the "spring switch" (ss) behind the roaring "Mammoth" of the rail world, so they could do their work.

No. 4056 (Ls-2 class 2-8-8-2): drivers: 57"; engine weight: 469,000 lbs.; steam pressure: 210 lbs.; tractive effort: 96,000 lbs.; superheated; Baldwin built: 1928; tender weight (loaded with 10,000 gal. of water and 16 tons of coal): 191,400 lbs.; engine & tender length: 99'2 1/16"; engine height: 15'5 5/16"; retired: Nov. of 1952.

*Credit: Photographer, Southern Railway; Curt Tillotson Collection.*

"fire-breathing," smoke-spewing Ls-1 class 2-8-8-2, No. 4020, heading to Appalachia, Va.- approximately two miles away- all at a "brisk" 25 m.p.h.

Unlike the more powerful, double-stacked Ls-2's, the older Ls-1's had only one, large smoke stack. The extra large front cylinders identified this "beast" as a compound Mallet. This meant the steam from the large boiler went straight to the smaller back set of cylinders. And what steam remained after the back pair was full, went to the front cylinders. As a result, it took larger cylinders to collect enough steam-"leftover" steam- in order for it to provide the power to enable the 2-8-8-2 to pull with all its might so the engine cold move its tonnage to its destination. The single expansion locomotive in which high pressure steam went to both sets of cylinders, proved to be more effective than the compound "giants."

Notice two things in this excellent photo: this "S" curve gives you a clear view at how the articulation worked as the upper part of the engine was rigid and did not move while the lower section-the drivers-followed the tracks. You can also see why the engine's headlight was placed just above the cowcatcher rather than the normal position on the front of the smoke box. The bottom part of the 2-8-8-2 turned as the drivers followed the tracks and the headlight gave the crew a constant look at the track. Whereas, if the light had been placed on the rigid upper part, it would not be able to highlight the track as the engine went around the curves.

The heavy snow actually enhanced the action of these mighty "stump pullers" doing their job. The mountains, sharp curves, grades, snow and coal movement were "home" for the powerful Articulateds which the Southern concentrated on the Asheville, Knoxville and Birmingham divisions.

Now, let's get back to our automobile and hope the car's heater works for, man, it's cold out here!

*Credit: Southern Railway Photo; Curt Tillotson Collection.*

No. 4020 (Ls-1 class 2-8-8-2): drivers: 56"; engine weight: 432,000 lbs.; steam pressure: 210 lbs.; tractive effort: 84,400 lbs.; superheated; Baldwin built: 1924; tender weight (loaded with 10,000 gal. of water and 16 tons of coal): 191,400 lbs.; engine & tender length: 97'8 1/4"; engine height: 15'5"; retired: Nov. of 1951.

Another Southern 2-8-8-2 pulling a long string of coal cars would mean another demonstration of steam power producing an unforgettable scene of rail drama. On this early, cold morning in Jan. of 1939, the magnificent example of power vs. heavy tonnage, gravity and even a heavy mountain snowfall was provided by a huge

A monster at rest! This photo allows us to have a close look at the biggest, most powerful class of steam locomotive owned by the Southern Railway System.

After bringing a long freight into Knoxville, Tenn., the huge Ls-2 class 2-8-8-2 traveled to the roundhouse. Here the massive Articulated, No. 4051, would be coaled, watered, inspected and, since this was a Southern locomotive, it would be washed and cleaned. Then a hostler would move the "big girl" to the ready track area where it would await a call to take on the mountains once again with tonnage tied to its tail-adding more revenue to the Southern's coffers.

The Articulateds proved to be the answer the Southern had been searching for in order to solve its problem of having to double-head most of their freight trains through the mountainous territory. The 2-8-8-2's helped to eliminate most of this costly practice. And the huge Ls-2's proved to be excellent "pushers" as well, using their 96,000 lbs. of tractive effort to help meet the numerous challenges found on the Asheville Division, especially the climb up mighty Saluda Grade. Just look at the size of this massive piece of steam motive power: twin stacks, the headlight placed above the cowcatcher where it would be able to illuminate the tracks continuously, even round curves. Everything about No. 4051 looked so right. This was one of the traits of Southern's steam power-esthetically pleasing, clean and in good operational conditions.

Soon the twin "shotgun barrels" would be blasting away through some of the most scenic territory in our country, creating a sight not soon forgotten, moving coal and general freight between Asheville, N. C. and Knoxville, where most of the Ls-2's could be found.

What stories No. 4051 could tell (if it could talk) about its constant combat against the Blue Ridge Mountains. The Southern made a wise investment in their 2-8-8-2's, especially the best of the lot: the Ls-2's.

*Credit: Photographer, Harold Vollrath; Curt Tillotson Collection.*

No. 4050 (Ls-2 class 2-8-8-2): drivers: 57"; engine weight: 469,000 lbs.; steam pressure: 210 lbs.; tractive effort: 96,000 lbs.; superheated; Baldwin built: 1926; tender weight (loaded with 10,000 gal. of water and 16 tons of coal): 191,400 lbs.; engine & tender length: 97'8 1/4"; engine height: 15'5"; retired: May of 1950.

Have you ever seen such a clean, impressive Articulated type of locomotive? Even for the Southern, known for the extra care it lavished on each and every one of its engines, this Ls-2 class of 2-8-8-2 was far more handsome than when it emerged from the erection shops at Baldwin in 1926. And talk about bridges! This freshly painted structure, with the road's name painted on its sides in impeccably clean white paint, was quite marvelous.

How could a railfan have such luck as to find a massive 2-8-8-2 "clean enough to eat off of" on an equally beautiful, sparkling bridge without anything to distract from this most outstanding exposure? Only one answer could possibly be for such "luck." It was a photo arranged by the Southern's public relations department-which it was. But, still, it was a most attractive representation of this railroad's motive power and an example of a road on its way to become one of the most successful (financial and otherwise) in the rail world.

Of all the Articulated engines the Southern had on its roster, it just happened to be No. 4050 on that bridge on this particular day? Could it have just been a lucky pick by the "PR" boys (it was an arranged event)? No. 4050 was the first of the road's 2-8-8-2's to be converted from a compound to a simple Mallet. Both sets of cylinders were of the same size and both received high pressure steam, making it far more efficient than the remaining 2-8-8-2's in the same series.

The photo was made near Cook Springs, Ala. (between Birmingham and Anniston, Ala.) on the Southern's main line between Atlanta and Birmingham in late March of 1926-shortly after the arrival of this new 2-8-8-2 from the builder.

What a magnificent view of the Southern's biggest class of steam motive power in its prime. Thank goodness, the "PR" crew decided to have this pose on film for all of us to see, including future generations of railfans.

*Credit: Southern Railway Photo; Curt Tillotson Collection.*

No. 4013 (Ls-1 class 2-8-8-2): drivers: 56"; engine weight: 432,000 lbs.; steam pressure: 210 lbs.; tractive effort: 84,400 lbs.; superheated; Baldwin built: 1918; tender weight (loaded with 10,000 gal. of water and 16 tons of coal): 191,400 lbs.; engine & tender length: 97'8 1/4"; engine height: 15'5"; retired: May of 1950.

Mountains and Articulated locomotives: the two terms were synonymous when it came to mountain railroading during the age of steam motive power. Indeed, grades, curves, coal and other tonnage were among the many reasons why the Articulated type of power was developed. They would reduce the costly practice of double-heading with smaller power; and, as a result, the roads would have more engines available to move more trains in "friendlier" territory.

The Southern received its first Mallets (most often called Articulateds) in 1909. Eventually, through improvements of these massive engines, the Southern helped to develop the Ls-2 class of 2-8-8-2's, a type which met all the parameters the road had set for mountainous operations.

An example of this "two engines into one" was shown here near Imboden, Va.-just north of Appalachia, Va.-this hot afternoon on July 29, 1949. No. 4013, an Ls-1 type of 2-8-8-2, and a graduate of the class of 1918 from Baldwin, would normally have a string of coal cars trailing its rear; however, today it had an easy job of pulling a local freight through the surrounding mountainous territory of the Southern's Appalachia Division.

Our photographer had to brave the heat, humidity, the poison oak, flies and snakes to make this impressive exposure. He found that No. 4013's fireman had all the steam the big 2-8-8-2 needed for this light work since some of it was escaping into the air through the "big girl's" safety valve. Note that the Ls-1's had one smokestack while the more powerful and younger Ls-2's were twin stackers. And, with the huge cylinders on the front and smaller pair in the middle, No. 4013 was a compound Mallet.

Even in mountain work, the Southern had graphite on the smoke box of No. 4013 and just look at the shine on its bell. No. 4013 had that recognizable "Southern touch."

*Credit: Photographer, August A. Thieme, Jr.; Curt Tillotson Collection.*

No. 4053 (Ls-2 class 2-8-8-2): drivers: 57"; engine weight: 469,000 lbs.; steam pressure: 210 lbs.; tractive effort: 96,000 lbs.; superheated; Baldwin built:1928; tender weight (loaded with 10,000 gal. of water and 16 tons of coal): 191,400 lbs.; engine & tender length: 99'2 1/16"; engine height: 15'5 5/16"; retired: Nov. of 1952 (sold to the Baltimore Steel Co.).

The two terms, "magnificent" and "action" can be defined in many ways. As a result, I will simply explain the terms by urging you to have a close look at this photo. Now, you have an idea-your own definition-of just what, to a railfan, the words "magnificent action," truly mean. What a superb scene of steam and steel at speed!

Who would have thought that a Southern Ls-2 class 2-8-8-2 could make such speed as demonstrated here in this excellent exposure of extra westbound No. 4053, shown here near Chattahoochee, Ga. pulling 65 cars filled with peaches, doing nearly 55 m.p.h. this morning on Aug. 25, 1946? The Southern already knew that their Ls-2 Articulateds, with their 96,000 lbs. of tractive effort, could move most any trains in the mountainous areas on the Asheville and Knoxville divisions. After all, the Ls-2's were the largest, most powerful steam motive power on the road's roster. However, who would believe those 16, 57" drivers could pull tonnage at 55 m.p.h.! Indeed, the engine rods were going up and down so fast that their "clanking" sounded like the firing of a machine gun.

The fireman spotted the photographer and he must have been a railfan himself, since he cut on his engine's stoker, resulting in a most photogenic appearance which heightens the already wonderful drama on this "hot" main line. The graphite covered smoke box and overall cleanliness of No. 4053 were typical traits for a Southern steam locomotive. One thing for sure, if the "big girl" continues to belch such heavy smoke, those white flags would not remain white in color much longer.

Now, hold onto your hat, make sure you have advanced your film and be sure to push your camera's shutter slowly, not allowing the fire-breathing monster approaching you at nearly a mile-a-minute pace to cause you to push your shutter too hard, resulting in an odd angle of your photo.

*Credit: Photographer, R. D. Sharpless; Curt Tillotson Collection.*

No. 4051 (Ls-2 class 2-8-8-2): drivers: 57"; engine weight: 469,000 lbs.; steam pressure: 210 lbs.; tractive effort: 96,000 lbs.; superheated; Baldwin built: 1928; tender weight (loaded with 10,000 gal. of water and 16 tons of coal): 191,400 lbs.; engine & tender length: 99' 2 1/16"; engine height: 15' 5 5/16"; retired: July 11, 1952 (scrapped at Haynes-Spartanburg, S. C.).

This is a steam locomotive pictured doing what it was designed to do and doing its job quite well, I might add.

When you mention an Articulated engine to a railfan, two things would probably come to mind: mountains and coal trains. This picture demonstrates both "things." Southern's Ls-2 class 2-8-8-2, No. 4051, was depicted north of Gate City, Va., pulling No. 83, a daily freight on the Appalachia Division, on a sunny but cold morning in Feb. of 1951.

Even on a regular run, all freights in the coal country would be found pulling a long line of empty hoppers back to the mines-as shown here in No. 83's consist-(I wonder how that lone box car got into this bunch of hoppers)-or lugging heavy coal trains out of the mountains.

The engineer and fireman were working as a team with the fireman keeping the boiler pressure up to 210 lbs. And the engineer, making sure his engine was using all of its 96,000 lbs. of tractive effort to keep the train moving, on big rails, in an area where the Ls-2's felt right at home: surrounded by mountains.

There were 45 empty hoppers plus a box and a caboose moving south at a good 25-30 m.p.h. pace in a most memorable fashion. One oddity, however, No. 4051, was one of the few Ls-2's with only one smokestack-the vast majority of this 2-8-8-2 class were "twin stackers."

Can't you hear that "stack talk," smell the coal smoke, feel a slight tremor in the ground and marvel at the "clanking" of the driver rods on this "two engines in one?" A scene such as this is always hard to put into words. As a result, let's just look at the photo and allow our imagination to do the rest.

*Credit: Photographer, Wayne Brumbaugh; Curt Tillotson Collection.*

No. 4013 (Ls-1 class 2-8-8-2): drivers: 57"; engine weight: 432,000 lbs.; steam pressure: 210 lbs.; tractive effort: 84,400 lbs.; superheated; Baldwin built:1918; tender weight (loaded with 10,000 gal. of water and 16 tons of coal): 191,400 lbs.; engine & tender length: 97' 8 1/4"; engine height: 15'5"; retired: May of 1950.

With the entire area surrounded by mountains, the unmistakable sounds of this local freight could be heard several minutes before it came into view since the "stack talk" echoed off the hills, time and time again, growing louder and louder. By the way, have you ever seen a local freight pulled by a massive 2-8-8-2? Well, here it comes: a huge Southern articulated (No. 4013) with all that 84,400 lbs. of tractive effort used in pulling 7 cars and a caboose near Imboden, Va. (not far from Appalachia, Va.) this July 29, 1949.

To see that smoke spewing off that single stack and hear the "shot gunning," you would expect to witness a long line of hopper cars, filled with coal, trailing behind the "beast from the Jurassic Era." With the numerous grades and curves so severe, Extra 4013 North still had to use some of its great power to pull this short local. No doubt, however, by tomorrow, this 2-8-8-2 would probably be used to haul coal, where its great power would be needed.

There was something special about mountain railroading. Because of the nature of the territory, you would expect to find the road's biggest motive power at work, creating scenes of smoke shooting skyward, driver rods "clanking," man and machine working together to overcome all the obstacles-natural and man-made-to get the tonnage to its destination. It took special engine crews to accomplish this feat. And, thank goodness, there were a few railran/photographers willing to travel to these isolated locations in order to record some of the most dramatic scenes so that others could enjoy the efforts of these brave souls and have a look at mountain railroading during the age of steam. It was truly a wondrous sight!

*Credit: Photographer, August A. Thieme, Jr.; Curt Tillotson Collection.*

No. 4051 (Ls-2 class 2-8-8-2): drivers: 57"; engine weight: 469,000 lbs.; steam pressure: 210 lbs.; tractive effort: 96,000 lbs.; superheated; Baldwin built: 1928; tender weight (loaded with 10,000 gal. of water and 16 tons of coal): 191,400 lbs.; engine & tender length: 99' 2 1/16"; engine height: 15'5 5/16"; retired: July 11, 1952 (scrapped at Haynes-Spartanburg, S. C.).

The Articulated locomotives were usually considered to be "beast of burden," lugging long trains (mostly of coal) and operating in the 15-20 m.p.h. range. True, they could pull almost anything a yardmaster would tie onto their rear; it was also true that their mighty tractive effort was used most efficiently at this range of speed.

When the Southern began to purchase the heavy and powerful 2-8-8-2's, they were not disappointed with the performance of their L-class steamers. They could really move the tonnage, helping to eliminate most of the costly practice of double heading trains with smaller power. In the case of the Ls-2's, the Southern discovered that their 2-8-8-2's of this class presented them with a bonus: they could not only pull tremendous tonnage but, on a comparatively level main line, they could move their train up to 50-55 m.p.h.!

Shown in this exposure of Extra 4051 East-made near Chattahoochee, Ga. on June 22, 1946, heading to Atlanta's Inman Yard-those 16, 57" drivers of No. 4051 were almost a blur and its driver rods were "clanking" so fast it looked (and sounded) like everything would fly apart due to its excessive speed. Those "mountain maulers" could, indeed, make good time on the main line.

What a sight: a huge 2-8-8-2 running eastbound on the main line between Birmingham and Atlanta with approximately 30 cars in its consist-all at nearly 55 m.p.h.! Thank goodness someone was there to make an exposure of this action since "seeing is believing." So, here is the photo, showing that an Ls-2 could really "pick 'em up and lay 'em down" when they were required to do so. Indeed, on the Asheville and Knoxville divisions, you rarely found a 2-8-8-2 exceeding 35-40 m.p.h., but on the Birmingham Division, they quite often broke "speed records" for these "beast of burden."

*Credit: Photographer, R. D. Sharpless; Curt Tillotson Collection.*

No. 4051 (Ls-2 class 2-8-8-2): drivers: 57"; engine weight: 469,000 lbs.; steam pressure: 210 lbs.; tractive effort: 96,000 lbs.; superheater, Baldwin Built: 1928; tender weight (loaded with 10,000 gal. of water and 16 tons of coal): 191,400 lbs; engine & tender length: 99' 2 1/16"; engine height: 15'5 5/16"; retired: July of 1952 (scrapped at Haynes-Spartanburg, S. C.).

Mountains, mountains, mountains! This was the place to be if you were a railfan with a camera during the steam era. Of course, you can still make excellent exposures of today's diesels in the hills; however, the drama produced by the "iron horse," working at full throttle with its stoker on, can never be reproduced by the "growlers."

Like in any location, however, there were numerous obstacles facing the railfan/photographer: in many scenic locations, you could not make exposures except during a few hours each day as a result of the shadows caused by the big hills. You had to be lucky, hoping a train would come by when the sun finally overcame those shadows. Then there were briars, poison oak, snakes and even the possibility of bears! Still, some of the most outstanding photos made of steam power in action occurred in the mountains.

A fine example of rail photography in the mountains is shown here as Southern's Ls-2 class 2-8-8-2, No. 4051, pulls the daily freight, No. 83, on the Appalachia-Bull Gap, Va. line, through Moccasin Gap-north of Gate City, Va.,-on a late afternoon in Feb. of 1951.

With 35 cars hung onto its rear (mostly empty coal hoppers), the big Articulated is shown heading upgrade with its stoker and sanders on, producing a dramatic representation of steam power vs. the mountains-truly, an unforgettable scene.

Look at that track! The ballast edges are as straight as a ruler. One reason why this was so was because a section crew-not machines-made sure "their" area of track was the best on the Appalachia Division.

My grandfather was a Southern track foreman; he and his seven man crew made sure that their section of track (from Stovall, N. C. to the N.C.-Virginia state line) was the very best on the East Durham, N. C. to Keysville, Va. line. Each section foreman and his crew took great pride in their work.

With the mountainous background, an Ls-2, 2-8-8-2 working full throttle with its stoker on-in the sun-moving over some of the most beautiful track you will find anywhere, you have a classic portrait of what it was like when the Southern's largest, most powerful class of steam power on its roster took on "mother nature" and gravity-magnificent!

*Credit: Photographer, Wayne Brumbaugh; Curt Tillotson Collection*

# Mighty Saluda Grade

When the Southern Railway was formed on July 1, 1894, it included all trackage of the large Richmond and Danville Railroad (often called the "Piedmont Air Line") and the East Tennessee, Virginia & Georgia Railway (nicknamed the "Kennesaw Route").

With all this mileage, the Southern became one of the largest lines in the South; however, it began to increase its length by merging, leasing or purchasing numerous other roads. Indeed, by 1917, it was a formidable railroad within our entire country. The Southern knew, however, that it needed additional connections to several other areas west of the Blue Ridge Mountains.

The Western North Carolina RR, which ran from Salisbury to Asheville, N. C. (140 miles long), was operational by 1879 and was leased to the Richmond & Danville in 1886. A second entry into Asheville was completed and operational in 1886 when the Asheville & Spartanburg RR completed its construction and was only 66 miles long. It became part of the R&D family in 1881-5 years before the line was completed.

Even though the Spartanburg & Asheville segment was much shorter than the route from Salisbury to Asheville-both Salisbury and Spartanburg connected with the Washington-Atlanta main line, it proved that being shorter did not necessarily mean being the most effective. True, the Salisbury entrance into the "Land of the Sky" (Asheville) involved some tough railroading, especially between Old Fort and Ridgecrest, N. C. with 7 tunnels and numerous sharp curves but they managed to keep the ruling at approximately 2%, while the road up from Spartanburg, S. C. had to face Saluda Mountain, meaning a 4.7% climb (for every 100 feet, the track rose 4.7 feet). This was a serious obstacle.

Unlike the Salisbury route where the engineers could keep the grades manageable with the tunnels and curves, the engineer's building out of Spartanburg did not have this luxury, for when they reached Saluda Mountain (32 miles from Asheville), they found, due to the geography of the area, that they could not go around or through it - they had to go over it! Thus, we had the steepest main line grade in the United States with that being the agonizing 4.7% climb (actually, near the town of Saluda, N. C., there were a few hundred feet where the grade reached 5.1%).

Heading toward Asheville, via Spartanburg, and facing a 4.7% grade, would require a large number of the Southern's most powerful locomotives with helper engines-at least between Melrose and Saluda, N. C. (a distance of approximately 3 miles). A long westbound freight would have to double and possibly triple the hill with helper engines (stationed at Melrose-the base of the hill) on all trips up Saluda Grade. And, if this was not bad enough, coming down such a steep grade was actually more dangerous than ascending this obstacle. In fact, so many railroaders lost their lives (27 by 1903) on runaway trains, that some suggested that this 66-mile line should be abandoned.

From Melrose, whose elevation was 1,494 ft. at sea level, rose to 2,095 ft. at Saluda! Eventually, the line received automatic block protection, braking systems were improved and the Southern had two safety tracks built which would divert a runaway train up a section of track with over a 10% grade and large amounts of sand covered these rails. One safety track was placed midway down the grade and the other was built at Melrose. Both safety tracks had their switches set for the safety run and a switch tender was stationed at both locations 24 hours every day. When a train was descending the grade and approaching a safety track, the engineer would blow his whistle in such a way that the switch tender knew the train was under control so he set the switch for the main line. These procedures stopped practically all the runaway problems. When C.T.C. (centralized traffic control) was introduced, the switch tenders were no longer needed since the dispatcher in Asheville controlled the switches. With the arrival of the diesels and their most effective dynamic braking system, the midway safety track was removed; however, the one at Melrose was never removed, even when the current Norfolk Southern recently terminated operations over the mountain. The tracks are still in place but no trains are heard fighting up the hill; no longer can you hear the loud "whine" of a down grade train's dynamic brakes-all is strangely silent today.

Even though Saluda remains quiet today, with the following photos, we have an opportunity to resurrect the past and see how it was during the exciting days of steam when it was a case of "muscles vs. gravity." The 2-10-2's and 2-8-8-2's - the largest and most powerful steam locomotive on the Southern's roster - were used to move the freights up and down the hill while the green and gold colored 4-8-2's handle the passenger traffic. All ascending trains had to have a helper engine, from Melrose, placed on the rear-or, on occasion, in front of the road engine-before taking on the mountain.

Look at the action and I think you will be able to hear the thunderous "shotgunning" of the most powerful engines in the Southern's stables. The ground was ankle deep in cinders and the rails were bleached white from all that sanding.

Now, let's take a look at the problems involved in moving trains up and down mighty Saluda Grade during the most dramatic era of steam operations.

ASHEVILLE 6

**HAYNE—B. I. TOWER—Westbound**

| Miles from Biltmore | Station Nos. | TIME TABLE NO. 7 In effect May 30, 1948 — STATIONS | FIRST CLASS 9 Daily | 27 Daily | SECOND CLASS 155 Daily | 157 Daily | 153 Daily |
|---|---|---|---|---|---|---|---|
| | | Lv | A.M. | P.M. | A.M. | A.M. | P.M. |
| 67.4 | 452 | W SPARTANBURG N | 8 20 | 2 15 | | | |
| 65.9 | 454 | (1.5) WYCHAYNE ...N | 8 25 | 2 30[156] | 1 50 | 10 40 | 4 00 |
| 65.5 | ...... | X (0.4) (E. End Double Track) | 8 31 | 2 31 | | | |
| 62.0 | W 62 | (3.5) SIGSBEE ... P (W. End Double Track) | 8 36 | 2 36[156] | 2 05 | 10 55 | 4 15 |
| 55.6 | W 56 | W (6.4) X... INMAN PNC | s 8 50[152] | s 2 45 | 2 20 | 11 15 | 4 30 |
| 52.2 | W 52 | (3.4) .... GRAMLING .. P | f 8 57 | 2 50 | | | |
| 49.3 | W 49 | W (2.9) CAMPOBELLO PD | s 9 03 | 2 55 | 2 35[158] | 11 45 | 4 50 |
| 44.4 | W 44 | (4.9) S. LANDRUM PD | s 9 12 | s 3 03 | 2 50 | 12 15 PM | 5 10 |
| 40.8 | W 41 | (3.6) .... TRYON .PD | s 9 20 | s 3 11 | 3 00 | 12 54[28] | 5 29 |
| 35.0 | W 35 | (5.8) WCXMELROSE ..N | s 9 35 | 3 28 | 3 30 | 1 15 | 5 45 |
| 31.9 | W 32 | (3.1) X... SALUDA ...N | s 9 50[154] | s 3 43 | 4 00 | 1 35 | 6 00[10] |
| 26.6 | W 27 | (5.3) .... TUXEDO PD | s10 03 | b 3 54 | 4 15 | 1 50 | 6 15 |
| 23.3 | W 23 | (3.3) .... FLAT ROCK PD | s10 12 | f 4 00 | 4 30 | 2 00 | 6 30 |
| 19.8 | W 20 | (3.5) WYX HENDERSONV'LE PNC | s10 32 | s 4 10 | 4 45 | 2 10 | 6 40 |
| 17.4 | W 17 | (2.4) .... SMYTH .PD | f10 37 | 4 15 | 4 55 | 2 20 | 6 50 |
| 14.2 | W 14 | (3.2) .... NAPLES ...P | f10 42 | 4 21 | 5 05 | 2 35 | 7 00 |
| 11.5 | W 12 | (2.7) .... FLETCHER PD | s10 48 | a 4 25 | 5 10 | 2 45 | 7 10 |
| 8.7 | W 9 | (2.8) .... ARDEN ..P | s10 54 | 4 32 | 5 20 | 2 55 | 7 20 |
| 3.1 | W 3 | (5.6) .. BUENA VISTA .P | f11 04[156] | 4 40 | 5 30 | 3 18 | 7 35 |
| 0.0 | S 139 | (3.1) Y BILTMORE.... | s11 14 | s 4 48 | | | |
| 0.1 | S 139 | X (0.1) B. I. TOWER .N (E. End Double Track) | 11 15[22][28] | 4 49[10][81][21] | 5 40[60][152] | 3 35[16] | 7 45 |
| 2 | S 141 | (1.9) WC ASHEVILLE .N Ar. | 11 30[22][28] A.M. | 5 10[21][50][81] P.M. | 6 00[60][152] A.M. | 4 00[16] P.M. | 8 00 P.M. |
| | | | Daily 9 | Daily 27 [10] | Daily 155 | Daily 157 | Daily 153 |

# SALUDA GRADE

ON THE SOUTHERN RAILWAY
BETWEEN MELROSE & SALUDA, N. C.

Map prepared from an aerial photo of a section of Polk Country, North Carolina. Photo by The Aerial Photography Field Office. Agricultural Stabilization & Conservation Service. U. S. Department of Agriculture. Salt Lake City, Utah 84130. Negative No. BOR-2JJ-316. 11-9-67.

Scale of photo: 1″ = 660′

REDUCED SIZE MAP ART
APPROXIMATE SCALE: 1″ = 2,092′

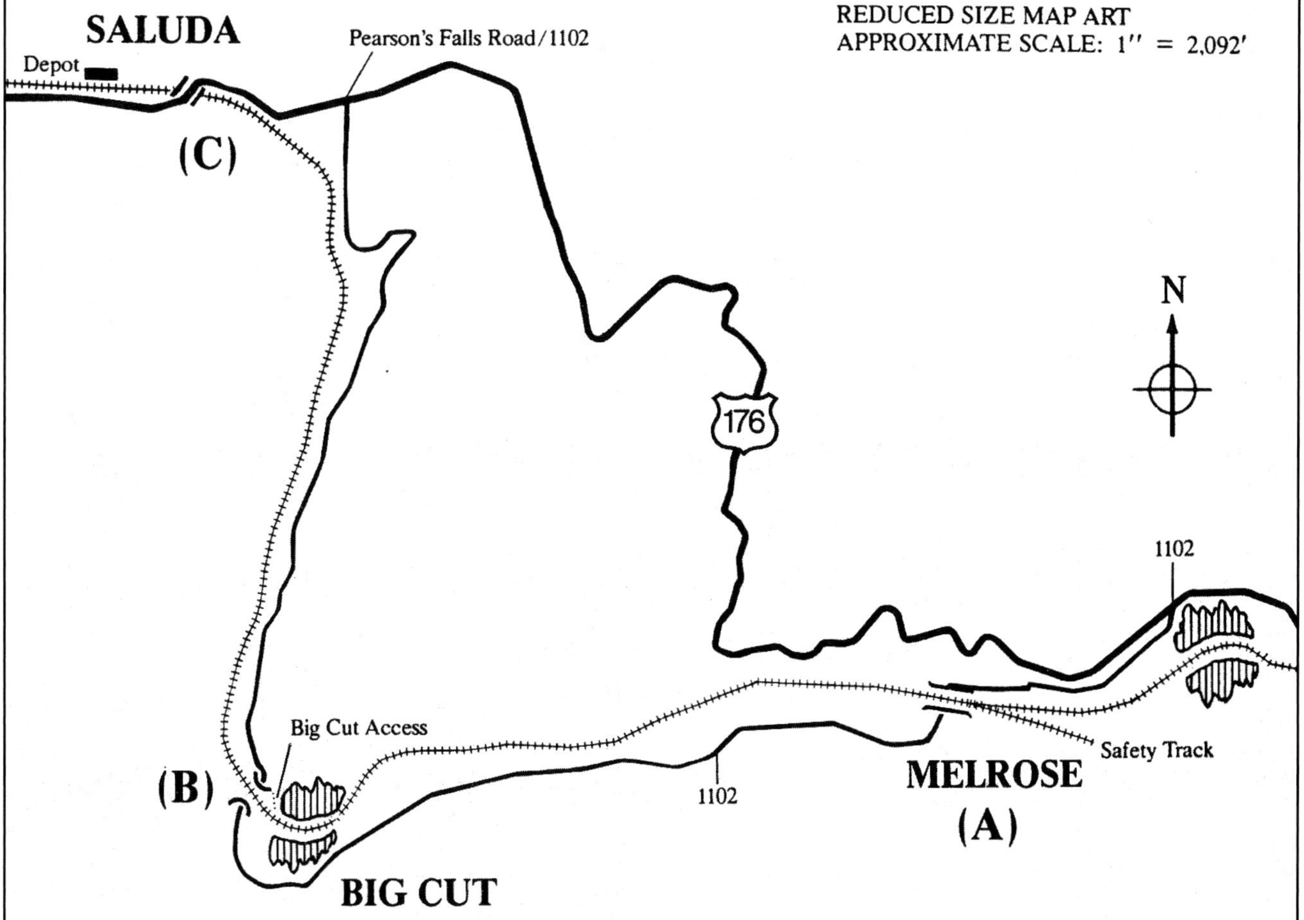

SALUDA
Pearson's Falls Road/1102
Depot
(C)
N
176
1102
Big Cut Access
(B)
1102
Safety Track
MELROSE
(A)
BIG CUT

## A SALUDA SHORT COURSE

For a quick visit to Saluda, the three best spots for viewing or photographing train activity are, in my opinion, (A) Melrose, (B) the Big Cut area, and (C) in and about the town of Saluda. These locations have merit because they are on safe terrain, are readily accessible, and provide a good overall view of activity. At Melrose, after a train is broken in half watch the engines depart with the first half. But don't tarry! Pass under the railway trestle staying on 1102, known locally as Pearson's Falls Road. When you reach a one-lane tunnel you are at Big Cut. On your right as you exit the north side of the tunnel is an access to Big Cut. Park, don't drive up. It is a short walk. Stay on the north side of the track so that you can get to your car quickly after the train passes. Next, proceed to the top to see the train arrive at Saluda. Follow the light engines back down to Big Cut and Melrose. Then start over again. At Big Cut, on the second trip up, cross over to the south side of the track and upgrade abit for a wider field of view. You'll have to wait for the train to pass but you'll still get to Saluda in time to make pictures west of town as the train leaves for Asheville. As with any rail action photography an advance drive over the route is desirable. And do try to check on schedules in effect at the time of your trip. Good luck. Have fun and remember that often repeated phrase—Safety First!

No. 5021 (Ss-class 2-10-2): drivers: 57"; engine weight: 367,000 lbs.; steam pressure: 200 lbs.; tractive effort: 73,600 lbs.; superheated; Baldwin built: 1917; tender weight (loaded with 9,000 gal. of water and 12 tons of coal): 171,000 lbs.; engine & tender length: 84 3 1/2"; engine height: 15'3"; Franklin lateral motion boxes on the front driver axles; Cole trailer trucks; retired: March of 1952.

Here, in this one photograph, was the essence of Saluda Grade during the age of steam!

Working up what is obviously a steep grade is a Southern Railway powerful 2-10-2, with its throttle wide-opened, sanders on and the fireman has the stoker open, throwing as much coal into the Santa Fe's firebox, in order to keep the steam pressure at 200 lbs. so the huge 2-10-2 can use all its 73,600 lbs. of tractive effort to keep the 1st section of through freight No. 157 moving towards Asheville, N. C. at 1:50 p.m. on a cool afternoon in Feb. of 1947.

No. 5021 is shown at 10-15 m.p.h., as it enters the area on Saluda Grade called the "Big Cut," cannonading on the steepest main line grade in the United States, with its "shotgunning" echoing off the surrounding hills. It was a sight and sound that would cause a viewer to have a rapid heartbeat, his adrenaline flowing through his system and to have cinders fall on him like rain.

This excellent exposure also helps to explain why so many railfans flocked to this area in order to record on film rail action that could rarely be found anywhere in our country. It was action that would stir one's soul, especially those fortunate enough to have been there in order to witness such a dramatic event unfolding right in front of them.

First No. 157 could be heard coming up the hill almost 20 minutes before the massive 2-10-2 heaved into view. At 4.7%, the 3 miles between Melrose and Saluda, N. C. pitted the biggest power on the Southern against this mighty grade and, as a result, creating such a spectacle that you almost had to see it with your own eyes to believe that such a scene actually occurred. Thank goodness, we have photos such as this one which captured such wondrous rail action so the rest of us can, at least, see what actually happened-day after day-during the time when steam ruled the rails and conquered Saluda Grade.

*Credit: Photographer, Wayne Brumbaugh; Curt Tillotson Collection.*

up a steep grade. The two safety tracks were designed to stop runaway trains heading down the 4.7% grade.

By just looking at these photos, you will see how the train and track in the photo to the left drops downhill at a steep angle. Yes, 4.7% was a torturous climb, indeed. And No. 4056 was making long, labored, extremely loud and impressive exhaust, shooting a large volume of smoke into the sky, with its throttle far back on its quadrant and you can see that the sanders were working as well.

In the photo below, you can really get a feel of how they kept going up and up and No. 4056, along with a huge 2-10-2 (No. 5021) pushing with all its might at the rear of through freight No. 157 on this late morning in Sept. of 1937, has 41 cars moving at a somewhat faster than a brisk walking pace. The ground was trembling, the blasting sounds of both the 2-8-8-2 and its 2-10-2 helper echoed off the surrounding mountains. With all that "wondrous" sound and the shaking of the ground, you knew that there was a battle going on, an all-out fight against the mountain. It was a conflict that occurred over a dozen times each day. And a descending train had its own "sounds," the squealing brakes and metal rubbing metal.

The Southern proved that with its 2-8-8-2's and 2-10-2's, they could succeed in getting tonnage and passengers over the 66 miles from Spartanburg, S. C. and Asheville, albeit somewhat expensive. And, between Melrose and Saluda, a memorable event occurred on each trip up and down the famous (some Southern officials might say infamous) Saluda Grade.

Mountain railroading: you've got to love it if you are a railfan!
*Credit: Photographer, Walt Thrall; Curt Tillotson Collection.*

"Coming and Going" - No. 4056 (Ls-2-class 2-8-8-2): drivers: 56"; engine weight: 469,000 lbs.; steam pressure: 210 lbs.; tractive effort: 96,000 lbs.; superheated; Baldwin built: 1928; tender weight (loaded with 10,000 gal. of water and 16 tons of coal): 191,400 lbs.; engine & tender length: 99' 2 1/16"; engine height: 15'5 5/16"; retired: Nov. of 1952; pusher: No. 5021.

The most powerful steam locomotives on the Southern's roster were the Ls-2-class 2-8-8-2's. Because of their awesome tractive effort-96,000 lbs.-they were frequent visitors to the Saluda Grade area. They, along with the Ss-class 2-10-2's, were among the major power which ruled the freight movements in this area for many years while the green and gold colored 4-8-2's handled the passenger runs-with the help of a 2-10-2 tied onto their rear end for the westbound runs up Saluda.

No. 4056 was captured on film in action, doing what it was designed to do. The twin-stacked 2-8-8-2 is shown adding to the deep amount of cinders already covering the area as it was approaching an automatic block signal, which indicated that Asheville was 33 miles away. Look closely over the first freight cars tied to No. 4056's tender and you will see the midway safety track, which headed

No. 5021 (Ss-class 2-10-2): drivers: 57"; engine weight: 367,000 lbs.; steam pressure: 200 lbs.; tractive effort: 3,600 lbs.; superheated; Baldwin built: 1917; tender weight (loaded with 9,000 gal. of water and 12 tons of coal): 171,000 lbs.; engine & tender length: 84' 3 1/2"; engine height: 15'3"; Franklin lateral motion driving boxes on the first set of drivers: Cole trailer trucks; retired: March of 1952. No 4056 was the leading engine.

With a massive 2-8-8-2 on the point of freight No. 157, 41 cars back we find a powerful Ss-class 2-10-2, No. 5021, using all its 73,600 lbs. of tractive effort to help No. 4056, with its 96,000 lbs. of t.e., in getting this struggling freight from Melrose to Saluda, N. C. and then on to Asheville (its destination) this late morning in Sept. of 1937, after passing the midway safety track.

This photo gives you an ideal look at just what kind of a grade a 4.7% really looks like. Moving this Asheville bound freight took all the power available to the Southern in order to overcome the gravity involved. From Melrose (with an elevation of 1,494 ft. of elevation) to Saluda (2,095 ft. of elevation), all within a 3-mile distance, took a great deal of raw muscle called "tractive effort" for a steam locomotive to accomplish its task.

You can see the smoke shooting skyward from the twin stacks of No. 4056-the most powerful class of steam locomotive owned by the Southern-while 2-10-2, No. 5021, had a fairly clean stack. The 2-10-2's fireman was a real "pro" since he was able to keep No. 5021's steam pressure at the 200 lb. level. Indeed, the "old girl" is shown with excessive steam coming out of its safety valve, so the 2-10-2 was doing all it could to help get No. 4056's train to the town of Saluda and then on to Asheville.

No. 5021 would uncouple from the train at Saluda, back downgrade to Melrose where it would receive more coal, water and sand, if need be; then wait for its next call to take on this steepest main line grade in the United States.

One definition of the term "rail action" could be put into two words: Saluda Grade!

*Credit: Photographer, Walt Thrall; Curt Tillotson Collection.*

No. 5035 and No. 5023 (Ss-class 2-10-2's): drivers: 57" (each); engine weight: 367,000 lbs. (both); steam pressure: 200 lbs. (both); tractive effort: 73,600 lbs. (both); superheated (both); Baldwin built: 1917 (both); tender weight (loaded with 9,000 gal. of water and 12 tons of coal): 171,000 lbs. (both); engine & tender length: 84'3 1/2" (both); engine height: 15'3" (both); Franklin lateral motion boxes on front driver axle (both); Cole trailer trucks (both); retired: Aug. of 1951 (both); pusher engine: No. 5047.

When the crews at Haynes Yard in Spartanburg, S. C. were putting together No. 157's train for Asheville, N. C., they realized that its tonnage would be greater than normal. Since No. 157 had to overcome Saluda Grade to reach its destination, the roundhouse crew did not send one but two, mighty 2-10-2's to pull this long train.

Even with a double-headed power consist, No. 157 would still need the assistance of the helper engine stationed at Melrose, N. C. (the base of Saluda Grade) in order to make it over the 3 miles of 4.7+% grade.

As a result, all the ingredients were in place to produce an even more dramatic scene than usual when No. 157 departed Melrose with three 2-10-2's, whose combined tractive effort was an incredible 220,800 lbs.! Believe it or not, all this power would be needed to reach Saluda, N. C.-the top of the grade.

The time was May 15, 1948-approximately 2:10 p.m.-as No. 157's lead engines, No. 5035 and No. 5023, came into view, approaching the area known as the "Big Cut," blasting for all their might as they took on this 4.7% obstacle (for every 100 feet the track rose 4.7 feet). Even though 4.7% did not sound too great, it had three behemoths down to 5-10 m.p.h. while they were all wide-opened. This event created one of those moments in rail history that could only be found at Saluda Grade in our part of the country.

Just feel the action: two powerful 2-10-2's working as hard as they could, dragging its tonnage in such a way that caused the ground to tremble, cinders were falling from the sky like sleet and the noise was tremendous. Even when these "beasts" had passed you, the sounds of another 2-10-2 (No. 5047) grew louder and louder, repeating the drama that had recently passed you, with the cinders and sand flowing freely as No. 157 approached the town of Saluda. Once there, No. 5047 would uncouple from the train, drift back to Melrose and wait for another battle with the mountain when an Asheville bound train arrived in its location.

For a railfan-even a "regular" person-it does not get better than this!
*Credit: Photographer, Frank Ardrey, Jr.; Curt Tillotson Collection.*

No. 5047 (Ss-class 2-10-2): drivers: 57"; engine weight: 367,000 lbs.; steam pressure: 200 lbs.; tractive effort: 73,600 lbs.; superheated; Baldwin built: 1918; tender weight (loaded with 9,000 gal. of water and 12 tons of coal): 171,000 lbs.; engine & tender length: 84'3 1/2"; engine height: 15'3"; Franklin lateral motion boxes on the front driver axle; Cole trailer trucks; retired: Aug. of 1951-No. 5035 and 5023 were on the front of the train.

Coming through "Big Cut," approximately halfway between Melrose and Saluda, N. C., the "Melrose Helper" is shown using all of its impressive 73,600 lbs. of tractive effort in order to get No. 157-a Spartanburg, S. C.-Asheville, N. C. through freight-to the top of this 4.7% grade and will continue to do so until the freight's 41 cars arrive in Saluda. Here this huge 2-10-2, No. 5047, would uncouple from the train and allow its two sister 2-10-2's (No. 5035 and No. 5023) to carry No. 157 on to its destination. Soon No. 5047 would drift back through this same location on its way back to Melrose where an inspection of the Southern's "big girl" would be made. And, if needed, the powerful 2-10-2 would receive more coal, water and that all-important sand (which helps those 57" drivers to maintain traction with those bleached white-colored rails) in order to be able to use all of its power in keeping the tonnage moving up the hill.

No doubt, within an hour or so, No. 5047 would be in the same area once again shoving another Asheville bound freight or possibly one of the four passenger trains that went up and down Saluda each day (No. 27 & No. 28-the "Carolina Special" and No. 9 & No. 10-the "Skyland Special").

Because of all the smoke coming from the road engines and helpers, the heavy sanding plus the brake shoe smoke created by downgrade trains, most of the day on Saluda Grade had a hazy appearance even though the sun was shining brightly. And the cannonading produced by the hard working 2-10-2's and 2-8-8-2's would echo off the surrounding hills long after the engines had passed your area.

This photographer had ample time to make these exposures this early afternoon on May 15, 1948 since the freights rarely moved over 10 m.p.h. And when a freight was too long and/or heavy that it had to "double the hill," i.e., it had to take half of the train to Saluda, return to Melrose and then bring the remainder of its consist to Saluda-where the train would be re-assembled before heading on to Asheville-there would be awesome sounds in and around the grade for a great deal of time; over an hour of rail action-intense rail action-would occur. As a result, you could stay busy photographing trains on this "steepest main line grade in the U.S.A." You could also record several downgrade trains as well, with that familiar sound of metal rubbing metal and the blue-colored smoke coming from hot brake shoes.

During the steam ere, the Melrose-Saluda area was truly a railfan's paradise!

*Credit: Frank Ardrey, Jr.; Curt Tillotson Collection.*

No. 5052 (Ss-class 2-10-2): drivers: 57"; engine weight: 367,000 lbs.; steam pressure: 200 lbs.; tractive effort: 73,600 lbs.; superheated; Baldwin built: 1918; tender weight (loaded with 9,000 gal. of water and 12 tons of coal): 171,000 lbs.; engine & tender length: 84'3 1/2'; engine height: 15'3"; Franklin lateral motion driving boxes on the first set of driver axle; Cole trailer trucks; retired: Dec. of 1951-No. 5029 was "pusher" engine.

You might wonder how the photographer was able to make such a remarkable photo of this heavy freight working up mighty Saluda Grade. No. 157, powered by Ss-class 2-10-2, No. 5052, had just passed the area known as the "Big Cut," and was approaching safety track No. 1-which was located approximately halfway up the grade.

The photographer climbed up the 10+% grade of the safety track and discovered that he had a perfect view of the main line. He knew a freight was working upgrade and it would be several minutes before it would come into view. As a result, he had ample time to reach this location-a place that proved to be a most outstanding site to record on film the coming of the Southern's big 2-10-2, using all its might. All this drama was occurring at approximately 5 m.p.h.

Look at the tracks-as white as snow, due to the sanding of thousands of trips up the grade over the years. The massive Sante Fe was shotgunning like cannons going off as it approached the safety track, moving slowly but still moving! There was an additional 2-10-2 on the rear of No. 157, pushing just as hard as No. 5052 was pulling; however, it was not yet in view.

A photo such as this could only be made during the winter months since the summer foliage would have made such a view impossible. So, even though it was a cold day in Dec. of 1947, it enabled him to make this unusual but excellent portrait of a battle with the 4.7% Saluda Grade. This was truly a rare and wonderful look at a most awesome spectacle of steam and steel takin' on the "hill:" A sight not soon forgotten!

*Credit: Photographer, Wayne Brumbaugh; Curt Tillotson Collection.*

No. 5029 (Ss-class 2-10-2): drivers: 57"; engine weight: 367,000 lbs.; steam pressure: 200 lbs.; tractive effort: 73,600 lbs.; superheated; Baldwin built: 1917; tender weight (loaded with 9,000 gal. of water and 12 tons of coal): 171,000 lbs.; engine & tender length: 84'3 1/2"; engine height: 15'3"; Franklin lateral motion driving boxes on the front pair of drivers: Cole trailer trucks; retired: Nov. of 1949 - No. 5052 was the lead engine.

After making an exposure of the front of this Asheville bound freight from a location on the steep incline of safety track No. 1 (shown at the top left of the photo), the photographer came down the hill in order to record the passage of the helper engine pushing No. 157 on the 4.7% grade.

With the train moving at 5+ m.p.h., the railfan had ample time to make an exposure of the lead engine, a big, burly Southern Ss-class 2-10-2, No. 5052, and then get down the steep hill of safety track No. 1 and pick a position where he would wait for the Melrose, N. C. based helper engine-another massive 2-10-2, No. 5029-to come into view. The powerful engine was really letting the world know that it was using every big of its 73,600 lbs. of tractive effort: along with a judicious amount of sanding to make sure its 57" drivers did not lose traction in its attempt to get this freight to its destination. The fireman had so much steam in this man-made beast, that some of it was escaping out of No. 5029's safety valve. Notice that the rail washer, located beneath the fireman's position, was operating in order to wash off the top of the rails.

With the stoker on, shooting smoke and cinders into the sky, the ground trembling under the 2-10-2's weight; the roadbed covered with cinders and the shotgunning exhaust echoing off the surrounding hills, we have an example of mountain railroading at its best.

In this instance, a picture is truly worth a thousand words! Enjoy!

*Credit: Photographer, Wayne Brumbaugh; Curt Tillotson Collection.*

No. 5027 (Ss-class 2-10-2): driver: 57"; engine weight: 367,000 lbs.; steam pressure: 200 lbs.; tractive effort: 73,600 lbs.; superheated; Baldwin built: 1917; tender weight (loaded with 9,000 gal. of water and 12 tons of coal): 171,000 lbs.; engine & tender length: 84'3 1/2"; engine height: 15'3"; Franklin lateral motion driving boxes on front set of drivers: Cole trailer trucks; retired: Dec. of 1951-"pusher" No. 5047 on the rear of the train.

Here is Melrose, N. C. during the steam era, located at the base of the 4.7% Saluda Grade. In the background, you can see the water tank plus safety track No. 2-both to the right of this train. The coal and sanding towers plus the little stations' semaphore signal are seen to the left of the freight. A "helper" engine was stationed at this location 24 hours per day, seven days a week. It would help the Asheville bound trains-both freight and passenger-up the 3 miles of grueling, struggling journey to Saluda, N. C. where the "helper" would uncouple from the train, drift back to Melrose and wait for the next westbounder (some would call them northbounders). There was also a short bridge just north of the station where both a creek and a narrow road passed under.

Once a freight arrived in Melrose, the "helper" would hook onto the caboose and then, with whistle signals, both engines would open up, gaining as much momentum as possible so as to get a good start before reaching the "you've got to see it to believe it" grade. If a freight was extra long, half would remain at Melrose while the front section went on to Saluda, N. C. Then both engines would return to Melrose, get the second part of the train and go back up the "hill" with all the fury and power that both engines could muster (this was called "doubling the hill"). Once in Saluda, the road engine would reassemble its train and head on to Asheville, while the "helper" would return to Melrose. Usually a Southern Ss-class 2-10-2 would be the "helper" although, on occasion, you might find a massive 2-8-8-2 doing the job, sitting at Melrose, waiting for its next call to go up the hill, pushing with all its might behind another caboose-now that was a sight and sound to behold!

No. 157, headed by Ss-class 2-10-2, No. 5027, is shown, wide-opened, at near 25 m.p.h., as it started the climb. You can just make out the smoke of "helper" No. 5047, another 2-10-2, south of the small station, also wide-opened. A battle had begun this early afternoon on May 15, 1948; and you will hear the fighting for 30-40 minutes. It was an experience that should be witnessed by all Southern steam fans. It would truly reinforce your love of trains. That's for sure!

*Credit: Photographer, David W. Salter; Curt Tillotson Collection.*

mighty Saluda Grade by itself. As a result, the "helper" engine stationed at Melrose 24 hours each and every day during steam operations, was assigned the job of helping No. 4538 up the 4.7% climb to Saluda, N. C. so it could continue working Southern's customers on the 66-mile Spartanburg, S. C. to Asheville run.

Up front of the local was a Light Mikado (No. 4538) which could muster 53,900 lbs. of tractive effort. Out of the Melrose "helper" siding rolled a massive Ss-class 2-10-2, No. 5021, ready to use its impressive 73,600 lbs. of t.e. to help the local. As I previously stated, this was truly a "Mutt and Jeff" power combination of engines. Still, the local reached Saluda and headed on to its next customer. We all know, however, where the majority of power originated to get this local over the 3 miles that boast the "steepest main line grade in our country"-that big, fat, powerful 2-10-2!

No. 4538 (Ms-class 2-8-2): drivers: 63"; engine weight: 272,900 lbs.; steam pressure: 200 lbs.; tractive effort: 53,900 lbs.; superheated; Baldwin built:1912; tender weight (loaded with 8,000 gal. of water and 12 tons of coal): 153,000 lbs.; engine & tender length: 77' 7/8"; engine height: 15'1 3/4"; built-up trailer trucks; retired: April of 1949.

If ever there was a "Mutt & Jeff" combination of motive power, this photo and its companion exposure has to be it. The northbound local freight arrived in Melrose, N. C. this August day in 1937 with too much tonnage for its Ms-class 2-8-2, No. 4538, to carry up

Shown here is the local's road engine negotiating the last curve as it approached the town of Saluda, putting all its 53,900 lbs. of muscle into this journey up the hill. The 2-8-2's volume of smoke and heavy (loud) exhaust almost matched that of the huge 2-10-2 just a few cars back, out of the photo. So, the "little guy" did his job (with the help of its much bigger "friend").

This unusual motive power combination just added to the mystic of Saluda Grade. We are fortunate that a photographer was there to record this unusual, but most enjoyable, movement.

*Credit: Photographer, Walt Thrall; Curt Tillotson Collection.*

No. 5021 (Ss-class 2-10-2): drivers: 57"; engine weight: 367,000 lbs.; steam pressure: 200 lbs.; tractive effort: 73,600 lbs.; superheated; Baldwin Built: 1917; tender weight (loaded with 9,000 gal. of water and 12 tons of coal): 171,000 lbs.; engine & tender length: 84'3 1/2"; engine height: 15'3"; Franklin lateral motion driving boxes on the first set of driver axle; Cole trailer trucks; retired: March of 1952-lead engine: Ms-class 2-8-2, No. 4538.

Coming around the last curve just south of Saluda, N. C., Southern's mighty Ss-class 2-10-2, No. 5021, is putting all of its 73,600 lbs. of tractive effort into its effort to help this Asheville, N. C. bound freight over the 3 miles of 4.7% to a brief section of 5.1% incline known as Saluda Grade this beautiful (and exciting) day in Aug. of 1937.

The powerful 2-10-2 was the "Jeff" in this "Mutt & Jeff" power combination moving up the hill. This was a local freight out of Spartanburg, S. C. that had too much tonnage to make it up the grade unassisted. The local's road engine, a light Ms-class 2-8-2, No. 4538 (the "Mutt" in our difference of engine sizes). The Ms-class "Mike" put out 53,900 lbs. of t.e.; with the 73,600 lbs. of tractive effort from No. 5021, the local made it into Saluda. There, No. 5021 would uncouple from the train, drift back to Melrose, go into the "helper" siding and wait for its next encounter with the "hill."

During the age of steam power, the Southern kept a 2-10-2 or, on occasion, a massive 2-8-8-2, stationed at Melrose 24 hours each and every day, since practically all trains needed help to overcome this impressive grade. This would also include the two passenger trains heading for Asheville each day: No. 28, the "Carolina Special" and No. 10, the "Skyland Special"-both with green and gold colored T-class 4-8-2's as road power.

The town of Saluda must have been the place to be during the era of steam. Hearing an upgrade train-with its motive power "down on its knees" at 5-10 m.p.h., a good 20 or more minutes before the "fire-breathing, steel monster came into town, must have been a most thrilling event to have experienced. And watching a train preparing to descend the precipitous 3-mile drop to the base of the hill from Saluda (with an elevation of 2.095 ft.) to Melrose (1,494 ft. of elevation), was awesome! Yep-Saluda was the place to be in the glory days of steam. You can still find an abundance of cinders in and around the tracks to this very day.

*Credit: Photographer, Walt Thrall; Curt Tillotson Collection.*

"Coming and Going"-No. 5045 and No. 5023 (Ss-class 2-10-2's): drivers: 57" (both); engine weight: 367,000 lbs. (both); steam pressure: 200 lbs. (both); tractive effort: 73,600 lbs. (both); superheated (both); Baldwin Built: No. 5045, 1918 and No. 5023, 1917; tender weight (loaded with 9,000 gal. of water and 12 tons of coal): 172,000 lbs. (both); engine & tender length: 84'3 1/2"(both); engine height: 15'3" (both); Franklin lateral motion driving boxes on front set of drivers (both); Cole trailer trucks (both); retired: No. 5045, March of 1950 and No. 5023, Dec. of 1951. No. 5047 was the pusher engine.

"Coming and going" — even for Saluda Grade, this was a most exceptional and thrilling movement: not one or two, but three hefty Ss-class 2-10-2's-two on the point pulling and one on the rear pushing-moving this extra north freight up this grueling climb from Melrose to Saluda, N. C. The sounds of their three exhausts were deafening, the trembling of the ground-resulting from this fight-must have registered on the Richter scale!

Southern's Ss-class 2-10-2's, No. 5045 and No. 5023, are using their combined tractive effort of an amazing 147,200 lbs. in getting this Spartanburg, S. C. to Asheville, N. C. freight up and over this 4.7% grade-all at 5+ m.p.h. The engine's stokers were on, the sanders working. The rail washer of No. 5023 was on so the "pusher" engine, No. 5047, would have better traction in order to use all of its 73,600 lbs. of t.e. to help its two "sisters" up front in reaching the town of Saluda-the top of the grade.

The two 2-10-2's on the point of this freight would continue on to Asheville from Saluda while No. 5047 would back down the mountain to Melrose where it would wait until called upon to head another train up the incredible 3 miles of extreme mountain railroading.

Looking at this action, can you imagine the sounds coming out of these two 2-10-2's with their throttles all the way back on their quadrants? Indeed, the action was so intense, it simply cannot be adequately described into words. It was one of those events in which you really had to be there in order to believe it and feel the full impact of such an awesome display of steam power.

The firemen were really earning their wages this hot September 16, 1948, as the two leading giants approach the area known as "Big Cut." It would take several minutes for the smoke from these powerful engines to dissipate. Just as it did, the "helper" power came by and filled the sky with more smoke. All the cinders coming out of the stacks of these behemoths were simply increasing the depth of those cinders already there-coming from thousands of similar movements up the grade over many decades of railroading.

No more words. Just look at this drama and draw your own conclusions as to what must have been going through the mind of the photographer as he recorded, on film, this unique scene of the Southern's constant struggle to get tonnage over the 66-mile route to the "Land of the Sky."

*Credit: Frank Ardrey, Jr., Curt Tillotson Collection.*

massive 2-8-8-2 in order to help those freight and passenger trains up the grueling climb over Saluda Grade. Even though this was the shortest distance from the Washington-Atlanta main line (66 miles from Spartanburg, S. C. to Asheville) while the second entrance from the east to Asheville was from Salisbury, N. C. (141 miles long), Saluda Grade was the greatest obstacle encountered on the route to the "Land in the Sky." Because of this fact, a majority of freight traffic went over the "Swannanoa Route." Still, there were several trains that took on Saluda which was protected by automatic block signals and there were two safety tracks in place to prevent damage and save lives by stopping any runaway trains going down this sharp drop from Saluda to Melrose.

No. 5047 (Ss-class 2-10-2): drivers: 57"; engine weight: 367,000 lbs.; steam pressure: 200 lbs.; tractive effort: 73,600 lbs.; superheated; Baldwin Built: 1918; tender weight (loaded with 9,000 gal. of water and 12 tons of coal): 177,000 lbs.; engine & tender length: 84'3 1/2"; engine height: 15'3"; Franklin lateral motion driving boxes on the first set of drivers: Cole trailer trucks; retired: Aug. of 1951; front engines, Ss-class 2-10-2's No. 5045 and No. 5023.

Here is a classic portrait of a huge "helper" engine pushing on the rear of a train, with all its might, assisting this freight in getting to its destination. And this "pusher" assignment was not just to get a train up just any grade, it was the steepest main line climb in the United States; it was the mighty Saluda Grade!

This massive Southern Ss-class 2-10-2, No. 5047, exerting all of its impressive 73,600 lbs. of tractive effort: providing just enough power to help two of its sisters on the point of this Asheville bound freight (No. 5045 and No. 5023) get from Melrose, base of the grade, up to Saluda-the top of the 4.7%-5.1% grade.

During the steam era, a powerful engine was stationed at Melrose, 24 hours each and every day-usually a 2-10-2 or, on occasion, a

That fireman on No. 5047 was lucky that his huge engine had a stoker and he was not required to hand-fire the monster. That was why his cap was still white! I often wondered why he turned around to look at the photographer. Did he think, "Why is that guy out in this wilderness?;" or possibly, "I'll get my picture taken;" or did he think the photographer was a Southern official watching his firing technique? Whatever was going through his mind, he had the "old girl" full of steam so it could accomplish the job. He also had the railwasher going at full blast while moving up the grade between 5-10 m.p.h. and showering the photographer with hot cinders.

It was truly a classic scene, thankfully captured on film so all of us can enjoy the excitement he must have felt, experiencing the thrill of being there, watching three, 2-10-2's taking on the mountain in this September 16, 1949, nearing the area known as "Big Cut." Magnificent!

*Credit: Photographer, Frank Ardrey, Jr., Curt Tillotson Collection.*

No. 5045 and No. 5028 (Ss-class 2-10-2's): drivers: 57" (both); engine weight: 367,000 lbs. (each); steam pressure: 200 lbs. (both); tractive effort: 73,600 lbs. (both); superheated (both); Baldwin Built: No. 5045 in 1918 and No. 5028 in 1917; tender weight (loaded with 9,000 gal. of water and 12 tons of coal): 177,000 lbs. (both); engine & tender length: 84'3 1/2" (both); engine height: 15'3" (both); Franklin lateral motion driving boxes on first set of drivers (both); Cole trailer trucks (both); retired: No. 5045-March of 1950 and No. 5028-July of 1952; "pusher" engine, No. 5025 (Ss-class 2-10-2).

This photo has it all. To me, it captures the essence of mountain railroading during the steam era in one of the most effective scenes I have ever seen!

Here we have an entire train-in one photo-leaving Melrose, N. C. this cold morning in Jan. of 1947, with three Southern huge Ss-class 2-10-2's, wide-opened, taking on a 4.7% grade for a three-mile climb to Saluda, N. C. The "helper" engine, No. 5025, was shown passing the little station at Melrose, producing a massive amount of both smoke and power and pushing for all its might the 25 cars of this extra north freight, headed by No. 5045 and No. 5028. Both the road engines and "helper" got the train up to 25 m.p.h. as a result of a slight dip in the track just north of Melrose. However, No. 5045 and No. 5028 had started up the grade (notice the rise in the track in front of the lead engines). By the time the "helper" engine passed the photographer, the speed had reduced to 10-20 m.p.h. and, as the railfan turned to watch this drama, the extra west was down into the 5-10 m.p.h. range and exerting a combined 220,800 lbs. of tractive effort to get the train over this grade.

Believe it or not but this scene would be repeated within an hour, for this photo shows the first part of the extra north working

the braking system of a downgrade train failed, it would usually result in a runaway train which caused a great deal of cost, not to mention loss of life.

Descending Saluda during the early days of operations caused so many deaths from runaway trains that several Southern officials actually considered abandoning the line entirely. Fortunately, in the early part of the 20th Century, improvements in the air braking system made them far more effective. And the Southern installed two safety tracks to help prevent these catastrophes. No. 1 safety track was placed midway down the grade while No. 2 was installed at Melrose, N. C. A "switch tender" was stationed at each safety track and the switch at both locations was always turned for the safety track which had a grade over 10% up the mountain with the rails covered with sand. When a train was descending the 4.7% grade, the engineer would use his whistle, blowing a special signal to indicate that his train was under control. When the switch tender heard that signal, he would line the switch for a main line movement.

Eventually the switch tenders were replaced by electronic devices after the line was equipped with automatic block protection. And when the diesels arrived with their excellent and effective dynamic braking, No. 1 safety track was removed. Only the one at Melrose remains and it is controlled by the dispatcher in Asheville. Runaways became almost a thing of the past.

Here we see Southern's Ss-class 2-10-2, No. 5017, heading down the hill with No. 154 at 11:30 a.m. in March of 1949. No. 5017 was on the approach to Melrose. Once there, the entire train would be inspected and the crew would allow the brake shoes to cool. Then, No. 154 would head on to Spartanburg's Haynes Yard and a connection with the Southern's Washington-Atlanta main line.

Just look at those rails. They show signs of extreme punishment from unknown number of battles with the pounding of the Southern's biggest, most powerful and heaviest steam engines in their "stables." And those rails really showed the results of these upward battles!

*Credit: Photographer, Wayne Brumbaugh; Curt Tillotson Collection.*

No. 5017 (Ss-class 2-10-2): drivers: 57"; engine weight: 367,000 lbs.; steam pressure: 200 lbs.; tractive effort: 73,600 lbs.; superheated; Baldwin built: 1917; tender weight (loaded with 9,000 gal. of water and 12 tons of coal): 177,000 lbs.; engine & tender length: 84'3 1/2"; engine height: 15'3"; Franklin lateral motion driving boxes on the first pair drivers: Cole trailer trucks; retired: March of 1950.

During the age of steam operation, we know how difficult it was getting trains over Southern's famous Saluda Grade. With a rise of mostly 4.7% and a few hundred feet of 5.1%, it usually required two, and at times, three of the road's powerful 2-10-2's to accomplish the job. Quite often the Southern even used the biggest, most powerful class of steam locomotive on their roster, the massive 2-8-8-2, to do battle with the mountain in a drama so impressive (and expensive for the Southern) that it drew railfans from all parts of the country to view and/or photograph this spectacular scene of steam and steel vs. the mountain.

Working upgrade against an incline so great was truly awesome. However, did you ever consider what it took to get a train down such a drop in elevation on a 3-mile run? Actually, descending Saluda Grade was far more dangerous than ascending this major obstacle. If

upgrade; all three 2-10-2's would drift back to Melrose from Saluda, get the remaining 25 cars of the train and then it would be fire, steam, steel and fury all over again.

Once in Saluda, after "doubling the hill," the head 2-10-2's would reassemble its train and continue its journey to Asheville. The "helper" returned to Melrose and awaited its call to do battle with the mountain once again.

I ask you, can you imagine seeing or (thankfully) photographing such action as this? Needless to say, it took our photographer several minutes to calm down, for this type of action was almost like having a narcotic "high," and, personally, I would not want to "kick" this kind of habit! This drama was truly one for Ripley's "Believe It Or Not!"

*Credit: Photographer, Wayne Brumbaugh; Curt Tillotson Collection.*

Today's local was powered by an Ms-class, light 2-8-2, No. 4505 and it only had 14 cars in its consist (several of those were empty). As a result, the powerful 2-10-2 stationed at Melrose would not be needed to get the local up to Saluda, N. C.

Shown approaching "Big Cut" No. 4505, which had a potpourri of cars in its consist, had its tonnage moving near 10 m.p.h. with a full head of steam for the attractive 2-8-2. In fact, the fireman had the "Mike" with so much steam, he had time to come over to the engineer side of the cab to "get into the picture."

The 2-8-2 might have been a light Mikado, but it was making the sounds and acting like its much bigger "sister" back at Melrose. The clanking of its main rods, the loud "crack" of its exhaust, all sounded like the 2-8-2 was heading up a big train.

Once in Saluda, its train would be inspected and if it needed any water there was a tank located in the town where it could quench its thirst. Then it would head on to Asheville while serving the Southern customers on the way.

It was an unusual sight to see such light motive power, unassisted, on the grueling 4.7% climb. Still, the 4500's were among the most esthetically pleasing of any 2-8-2 to ride the rails. As a result, it was an excellent opportunity to make a portrait of the little "Mike" conquering mighty Saluda Grade!

No. 4505 (Ms-class 2-8-2): drivers: 63"; engine weight: 272,900 lbs.; steam pressure: 200 lbs.; tractive effort: 53,900 lbs.; superheated; Baldwin Built: 1911; tender weight (loaded with 8,000 gal. of water and 12 tons of coal): 153,000 lbs.; engine & tender length: 77' 7/8"; engine height: 15'1 3/4"; built-up trailer trucks; retired: April 3, 1952 (sold to the Baltimore Steel Co.).

It was 11:10 a.m. on the morning of April 15, 1948, near Melrose, N. C.-at the base of Saluda Grade. And there was a lull in traffic both up and down the grade. So, it was an ideal time for the Spartanburg, S. C. to Asheville, N. C. local freight, running as Extra 4505 North, to head up the hill.

*Credit: Photographer, Unknown; Curt Tillotson Collection.*

No. 5045 and No. 5028 (Ss-class 2-10-2's): drivers: 57" (both); engine weight: 367,000 lbs. (both); steam pressure: 200 lbs. (both); tractive effort: 73,600 lbs. (both); superheated (both); Baldwin Built: No. 5045 in 1918 and No. 5028 in 1917; tender weight (loaded with 9,000 gal. of water and 12 tons of coal): 171,000 lbs. (both); engine & tender length: 84'3 1/2" (both); engine height: 15'3" (both); Franklin lateral motion driving boxes on first set of drivers (both); Cole trailer trucks (both); retired: No. 5045 in March of 1950 and No. 5028 in July of 1952; "pusher" engine: No. 5035.

This is it! The curtain rises and the play begins. The stars of this production

No. 4021 (Ls-2 class 2-8-8-2): drivers: 56"; engine weight: 469,000 lbs.; steam pressure: 210 lbs.; tractive effort: 96,000 lbs.; superheated; Baldwin Built: 1926; tender weight (loaded with 10,000 gal. of water and 16 tons of coal): 191,400 lbs.; engine & tender length: 99'2 1/10"; engine height: 15'5 5/16"; retired: Nov. of 1952 (sold to the Baltimore Steel Co.).

It was always a special occasion on Saluda Grade when the Southern's most powerful and heaviest class of steam locomotive, the mighty Ls-2 class 2-8-8-2's (in this case it was No. 4021), took on the "hill."

The twin-stack's exhaust sounded like a double barrel shotgun going off repeatedly, the four main driver rods were "clankin" so loud that you felt they would drop off at anytime and that impressive 96,000 lbs. of tractive effort was being used to conquer this major obstacle on the Spartanburg, S.C. to Asheville, N.C. main line. This type of "twin stacked" action would even draw the attention of many of the citizens of Saluda, N. C. who were used to this continuous fight up the 4.7% grade (now could anyone get used to this type of dramatic struggle?).

Extra 4021 North was shown nearing the top of the grade at Saluda-just above Safety Track No. 1-this cold Dec. of 1947 morning. Even with all its power, the Extra North required the help of a big Ss-class 2-10-2, No. 5028, pushing on its rear (note No. 5028's smoke above the hill to the right of the train).

What a sight! What a sound! All this power and it was making between 5-10 m.p.h. Notice how the smoke was going straight up-a sure sign that the engine was really working hard at a slow rate of speed, but it was still moving!

The engineer knew that regardless of its slow pace, No. 4021 would keep moving, especially since the big 2-10-2 on the rear using all of its 73,600 lbs. of t.e. to make sure the freight made it to Saluda. By the way, No. 4021 was one of the few compound Mallet to be converted to a simple articulated which gave it an increased in tractive effort.

Looking at this massive 2-8-8-2 with its stoker on and shouting to "high heaven," it appeared that the 2-8-8-2 was right where it belonged-in the mountains, working the grades.

A mystery: how could those flags be so clean and white with all that smoke, steam and road grime all around?

*Credit: Photographer, Wayne Brumbaugh; Curt Tillotson Collection.*

are three heavyweight, man-made monsters and a mountain. It would be a soul-stirring performance that a Hollywood director would wish he could produce.

Here is the plot for the play: two of Southern's huge Ss-class 2-10-2's (No. 5045 and No. 5028) are shown wide-opened, using all their 73,600 lbs. of tractive effort to gain as much momentum as possible leaving Melrose, N. C. and, with the help of an additional 2-10-2 hooked onto the rear of the train (notice its smoke in the background), it would take the power of all three massive Santa Fe class steamers to take on the steepest main line grade in our country, a three-mile climb. A short distance, true, but it would involve a struggle up a 4.7% grade with a short section of 5.01% for good measure. The combined might of these powerful locomotives to get this Extra 5045 North up and over this obstacle and into Saluda, N. C.-all at a speed of between 5-10 m.p.h. this hot afternoon (2:10 p.m.) on Sept. 16, 1948-would be needed!

The fight against gravity would consume a large amount of coal, water, a judicious amount of sanding and all the experience possible from these three engine crews to make it successfully over this mountain-and they would make it!

Believe it or not but this was a common occurrence between Melrose and Saluda during the day when steam ruled the mountains. It was thrilling, exciting, traumatic-there are simply not enough words available to adequately describe such a magnificent event.

Yes, this was a play and it could not have been more dramatic if a Hollywood director had planned it himself. It was the Southern's excellent fleet of steam locomotives in action, doing what they were designed to do and doing it quite well. In fact, this "play" deserved an Academy Award for its performance. Of this fact there can be no doubt: Saluda Grade + 2-10-2's + freight tonnage = a moment in rail history that could never be forgotten. With such photos as this, it will never, ever be forgotten!

Take a bow Nos. 5045, 5028 and 5035 (the "pusher"), for a job well done!

*Credit: Photographer, Frank E. Ardrey, Jr.; Curt Tillotson Collection.*

No. 4050 (Ls-2 class 2-8-8-2): drivers: 56"; engine weight: 469,000 lbs.; steam pressure: 210 lbs.; tractive effort: 96,000 lbs.; superheated; Baldwin Built: 1926; tender weight (loaded with 10,000 gal. of water and 16 tons of coal): 191,400 lbs.; engine & tender length: 99'2 1/16"; engine height: 15'5 5/16"; retired: Nov. of 1952.

If ever there was a photograph that demonstrated the awesome effects of a 4.7% grade which trains had to climb or descend, this is it! Look at the tracks and notice how they seem to go down and down, disappearing from sight! Now, imagine having to get a long, heavy freight up such an obstacle-which ran for 3 miles-Wow! This explains why the Southern had to marshal its heaviest and most powerful steam power in this area in order to take on the "hill."

Here we have an excellent example of just what it took to overcome this "steepest main line grade in the United States." In this case, 1st No. 151 is shown entering the town of Saluda, N. C.-the top of the grade-with a massive Ls-2 class 2-8-8-2, No. 4050, shotgunning with its "double-barrel" stacks, shaking the entire town with its tremendous weight and 96,000 lbs. of tractive effort-all at 5 m.p.h.!

You simply cannot put into words the actual sounds, the smells and the rumbling going on in this amazing spectacle of mountain railroading, especially during the era of steam operations. If you were not there to experience this drama in person, photos such as the one used here will have to suffice.

Even with all its enormous power, No. 4050 had to have the help of a huge 2-10-2 that was stationed at Melrose, N. C.-the base of the grade, which was hooked onto the rear of 1st No. 151 and its hard working road engine.

Just imagine living in Saluda during the steam era and experiencing such sights as this train-which you could hear approaching your location at least 20 minutes before this "behemoth" crawled into view-which occurred twelve or more times each day and night plus hearing the "squeal" of brake shoes from those numerous trains that descended Saluda Grade. I know one thing for sure. If I lived in Saluda at this time, I would probably go broke very soon as I would be purchasing rolls and rolls of film, then have them processed and finally have them enlarged-this would cost a great deal of financing, eventually causing me to "go broke."

Still, I would truly be in "rail heaven" if I could see such action as shown here this cloudy morning of Nov. of 1947, over and over again, day after day. It would truly be a "Shangri-La" for a railfan!

*Credit: Photographer, Wayne Brumbaugh; Curt Tillotson Collection.*

No. 5045 (Ss-class 2-10-2): drivers: 57"; engine weight: 367,000 lbs.; steam pressure: 200 lbs.; tractive effort: 73,600 lbs.; superheated; Baldwin built: 1918; tender weight (loaded with 9,000 gal. of water and 12 tons of coal): 171, 000 lbs.; engine & tender length: 84' 3 1/2"; engine height: 15'3"; Franklin lateral motion boxes on the front set of drivers: Cole trailer trucks; retired: March of 1950.

When steam ruled Saluda Grade, the Southern stationed a "helper" engine at Melrose, N. C.-the base of the 4.7%, 3-mile climb to Saluda, N. C. This procedure was necessary since practically every train heading for Asheville, N. C. from Spartanburg, S. C. would need help in getting up this grueling climb, no matter how powerful the road engine might be.

Melrose had a water tank, a coaling and sanding facility; this was the main line, a "runaround" track, a regular siding, Safety Track No. 2 (to help stop a possible downgrade runaway train) plus a small building I would call a station.

When an Asheville-bound freight arrived, the "helper" engine would usually go to the rear of the train, couple to its caboose and, with whistle communications, the "helper" would start shoving with all its might while the road engine would start pulling. Since there was a small, short drop in the track leaving Melrose, both engines would try to gain as much momentum as possible-usually 25 m.p.h.-before reaching the "hill." By the time the train arrived in Saluda, the speed would usually be in the 5-10 m.p.h. range. After arriving in town, the "helper" would drift back to Melrose and wait for its next call to take on the mountain. If a freight was too long, they would have to "double the hill, i.e., take half of the tonnage to Saluda, return to Melrose and bring the remaining cars up the hill once more. The road engine would reassemble the train and head on to Asheville while the "helper" went back to Melrose. On occasion, the tonnage was so great it would have to "triple" the climb. Even passenger trains needed assistance up the grade. There was seldom a dull moment at Melrose.

Shown here is "helper" No. 5045, a big Southern Ss-class 2-10-2, returning to Melrose after helping a train up the grade this April of 1947 afternoon. Most often, a 2-10-2 did the work from Melrose to Saluda, using every ounce of its 73,600 lbs. of tractive effort to get the job done. On occasion, you might find a massive 2-8-8-2 as a "helper." With its impressive 96,000 lbs. of t.e., this class of steam locomotive was the most powerful steam engine on the Southern's roster.

Here is where the continuous, never-ending battle of steam and steel vs. the mountain began. The people in Saluda could hear the fight begin almost 20 minutes before the train heaved into view. And at Melrose, you could hear the "squealing" of brake shoes and see all the smoke from the hot brakes long before a Spartanburg bound train arrived. The downgrade train would have a thorough inspection and it would wait long enough to allow its brakes to cool off. Then the train would continue its journey to Haynes Yard in Spartanburg.

Yes, Melrose was the place to be in order to watch the "big boys" preparing for battle. These were truly the "good old days!"

*Credit: Photographer, Unknown; Curt Tillotson Collection.*

# The Swannanoa Route

During the days of the Southern Railway System, one of the major connections between the eastern and western portions of the system was the Asheville Division's Salisbury-Asheville, N. C. line (141 miles in length).

As this strategic segment of the Southern departed Salisbury, you were still in North Carolina's Piedmont region where gentle rolling hills were the norm and did not present any trouble for the trains operating westbound on this automatic block protected route. However, once you arrived in Marion, N. C. (99 miles from Salisbury), the hills became more frequent and steeper. And, off to the west you could see a long line of mountains covering the entire horizon. When you reached Old Fort, N. C. (111 miles from Salisbury) that long line of hills became a tremendous, threatening wall call the Blue Ridge Mountains. You knew that some difficult railroading would be encountered; and, to reinforce this fact, there was usually a heavy, huge and powerful 2-10-2 Santa Fe waiting at Old Fort in order to assist almost all freights (and some of the passenger trains with more cars in their consist than usual) on their westbound journey through that "wall" and over the mountains. Since the elevation in Salisbury was near 875 ft. above sea level, while Asheville's elevation was 2,288 ft., the 2-10-2's were needed to reach the "Land of the Sky," i.e., Asheville.

To arrive at Ridgecrest, N. C. (3.4 miles "as the crow flies") it took the engineers who laid down the line, to take 12 miles, 7 tunnels and numerous curves to reach Ridgecrest and keep the grade under 2%. The accompanying map will identify the tunnels and their length, the types of curves encountered plus how far these locations were from Salisbury (enclosed in a circle).

Even though the second line into Asheville (from Spartanburg, S. C.) was shorter in mileage, it had a major obstacle that all trains bound for Asheville had to overcome: Saluda Grade-at 4.7%, it was the steepest main line grade in the country. Because of this tremendous problem, the vast majority of freights coming into and out of Asheville used the "Swannanoa Route" from Salisbury. Concerning scenery, the Salisbury-Asheville line featured one of the most awe-inspiring vistas of mountain beauty as well. I was fortunate enough to ride both routes in passenger trains and, as a result, I would support this statement.

When you mention "mountains" to a railfan, the first thing that would come to mind would be BIG motive power. This would be a correct assumption. Powerful Ss-class 2-10-2's were the most common steam power on both routes. As mentioned previously, a 2-10-2 would either couple to the road engine or hook onto the caboose of a westbound freight at Old Fort in order to get the tonnage over those grueling, but most photogenic, 12 miles.

Because of the numerous sharp curves encountered on the "Swannanoa Route," most locomotives-especially the 2-10-2's and even the green and gold colored 4-8-2's, which moved the passenger trains-were equipped with Franklin lateral motion devices on the front pair of drivers in order to reduce damage to the engine flanges and rails on their many curves. The largest and most powerful steam locomotives on their roster, the 2-8-8-2 Articulateds, were restricted from the Salisbury line because of their extra long engine frame. They were used, with great effect, fighting Saluda Grade. Local freights could be powered by either 2-8-0 Consolidations or 2-8-2 Mikados; however, due to their short engine bases, they could travel the line without any major problems, although if they had too much tonnage on their westbound journey, they might need the help of a "BIG" friend from Old Fort to help them conquer those 12 treacherous miles.

Now, look at the following photos and see why railfans flocked to these locations, for dramatic action was commonplace in mountain railroading, especially during the steam era. One other thing: watch out for the snakes!

ASHEVILLE 4 — SALISBURY—ASHEVILLE—Westbound

| Capacity of Tracks in Cars. Siding | Other | TIME TABLE NO. 7 In effect May 30, 1948 — STATIONS | SECOND CLASS 81 Daily | 65 Ex. Sun. | 61 Ex. Sun. | 63 Ex. Sun. | 53 Daily | | 55 Daily | 59 Daily | |
|---|---|---|---|---|---|---|---|---|---|---|---|
| | | Lv. | A.M. | A.M. | A.M. | P.M. | P.M. | | P.M. | P.M. | |
| ...... | Yard | WYX. SALISBURY .....N | 6 45[55] | 7 00[81] | ........ | ........ | 2 45[54] | ........ | 9 00 | ........ | ........ |
| 56 | | 5.0 ....... MAJOLICA ....P (West End Double Track) | 7 00 | 7 15 | ........ | ........ | 2 55[54] | ........ | 9 10 | ........ | ........ |
| 58 | 140 | 6.4 WYX.. BARBER ......N | 7 15 | 7 30 | ........ | ........ | 3 06 | ........ | 9 25 | ........ | ........ |
| 36 | 11 | 2.0 ....... CLEVELAND .....P | 7 20 | 7 45 | ........ | ........ | 3 10 | ........ | 9 30 | ........ | ........ |
| E 62 W61 | 10 | 5.0 ....... ELMWOOD .....P | 7 35 | 8 00 | ........ | ........ | 3 21[22] | ........ | 9 45 | P.M. | ........ |
| 58 | 160 | 7.2 WYX STATESVILLE ....N | 7 50 | 8 38 | ........ | ........ | 3 40 | ........ | 10 05[50] | 11 00[58] | ........ |
| 71 | 6 | 7.2 ........ EUFOLA .......P | 8 28 | 9 25[52] | ........ | ........ | 3 52 | ........ | 10 20 | 11 13 | ........ |
| 77 | 10 | 5.6 ....... CATAWBA ...PD | 9 10[52] | 9 43 | ........ | ........ | 4 02 | ........ | 10 31[58] | 11 23 | ........ |
| 61 | 5 | 4.1 ...... CLAREMONT ...P | 9 20[64] | 10 18[11] | ........ | ........ | 4 11 | ........ | 10 40 | 11 30 | ........ |
| 63 | 40 | 5.7 X W.. NEWTON .....N | 9 35 | 11 55 | ........ | ........ | 4 23 | ........ | 10 51 | 11 55 | ........ |
| ...... | 10 | 1.7 ..... CONOVER ........ | ........ | ........ | ........ | ........ | ........ | ........ | ........ | ........ | ........ |
| 89 | ...... | 4.1 ........ OYAMA .....P | 9 48 | 12 30[54] PM | ........ | ........ | 4 35[56] | ........ | 11 02 | 12 07 AM | ........ |
| 61 | 126 | 3.6 X..... HICKORY .....N | 10 00 | 12 40 | ........ | ........ | 4 42 | ........ | 11 12 | 12 15 | ........ |
| 71 | 7 | 4.7 ...... HILDEBRAN ..PD | 10 15 | 1 00 | A.M. | ........ | 4 55[12] | ........ | 11 23 | 12 25 | ........ |
| E 85 W82 | 45 | 5.6 WYCX CONNELLY SPRINGS ..N | 10 30 | 1 20[22] | 7 00[64] | ........ | 5 07 | ........ | 11 35 | 12 37[52] | ........ |
| ...... | 23 | 3.0 ....... VALDESE ....... | ........ | P.M. | ........ | ........ | ........ | ........ | ........ | ........ | ........ |
| 67 | 12 | 3.1 ........ DREXEL ....PD | 10 50[54] | ........ | 7 40[52] | ........ | 5 15 | ........ | 11 47 | 12 50 | ........ |
| 67 | 120 | 4.5 X.... MORGANTON ....N | 11 00 | ........ | 8 10[62] | ........ | 5 30 | ........ | 11 57[52] | 12 59 | ........ |
| 61 | 20 | 6.0 ...... GLEN ALPINE ..PD | 11 15 | ........ | 8 50 | ........ | 5 40[16] | ........ | 12 09 AM | 1 12 | ........ |
| 72 | 15 | 4.9 W.. BRIDGEWATER ..P | 11 45 | ........ | 9 20 | ........ | 6 02 | ........ | 12 19 | 1 21 | ........ |
| 60 | 8 | 4.9 .......... NEBO .......P | 12 01 PM | ........ | 9 58[54] | ........ | 6 12 | ........ | 12 29 | 1 30 | ........ |
| ...... | 52 | 3.5 X ... CLINCHCROSS ...... | ........ | ........ | ........ | ........ | ........ | ........ | ........ | ........ | ........ |
| 60 | 124 | 1.9 YW.. MARION ......N | 12 49[11][22] | ........ | 10 35 | ........ | 6 23 | ........ | 12 40 | 1 42 | ........ |
| 61 | 6 | 5.7 ....... GREENLEE .....P | 1 23 | ........ | A.M. | ........ | 6 35 | ........ | 12 52 | 1 53 | ........ |
| E 66 W65 | 45 | 5.7 WYX.. OLD FORT ....N | 2 37[56] | ........ | ........ | ........ | 7 14[50] | ........ | 1 05 | 2 20 | ........ |
| 85 | ...... | 3.9 ....... DENDRON .....P | 3 00[12] | ........ | ........ | ........ | 7 32[58] | ........ | 1 21 | 2 36 | ........ |
| E 81 W68 | 5 | 4.2 ....... COLEMAN ....P | 3 20 | ........ | ........ | P.M. | 7 50 | ........ | 1 41 | 2 53 | ........ |
| 59 | 23 | 4.0 WYCX RIDGECREST ....N | 3 38 | ........ | ........ | 12 40 | 8 10 | ........ | 2 00 | 3 09 | ........ |
| 60 | 15 | 1.9 ... BLACK MOUNTAIN P | 3 45 | ........ | ........ | 1 00 | 8 20 | ........ | 2 10 | 3 15 | ........ |
| E 57 W71 | 26 | 4.7 WX.. SWANNANOA ..PD | 3 55 | ........ | ........ | 1 30 | 8 30 | ........ | 2 25 | 3 30 | ........ |
| 56 | 15 | 4.5 ........ AZALEA ....PD | 4 01[16] | ........ | ........ | 1 45 | 8 45 | ........ | 2 40 | 3 55 | ........ |
| ...... | Yard | 4.7 X Y ..BILTMORE ....... | ........ | ........ | ........ | ........ | ........ | ........ | ........ | ........ | ........ |
| ...... | Yard | 0.1 .... B. I. TOWER .....N (East End Double Track) | 4 30[10][27] | ........ | ........ | 2 00[11][12] | 9 00[82] | ........ | 3 00 | 4 08[52] | ........ |
| ...... | Yard | 1.9 WC ASHEVILLE .....N Ar. | 4 45[21][27][21] | ........ | ........ | 2 20[11][12] | 10 00 | ........ | 4 00[52][89] | 4 15[52][55] | ........ |
| | | | P.M.[10] | P.M. | A.M. | P.M. | P.M. | | A.M. | A.M. | |
| | | | Daily 81 | Ex. Sun. 65 | Ex. Sun. 61 | Ex. Sun. 63 | Daily 53 | | Daily 55 | Daily 59 | |

Right: Map-Old Fort to Swannanoa, N. C. — including tunnels and mile posts.

*Credit: Map, Ray Carneal; Curt Tillotson Collection.*

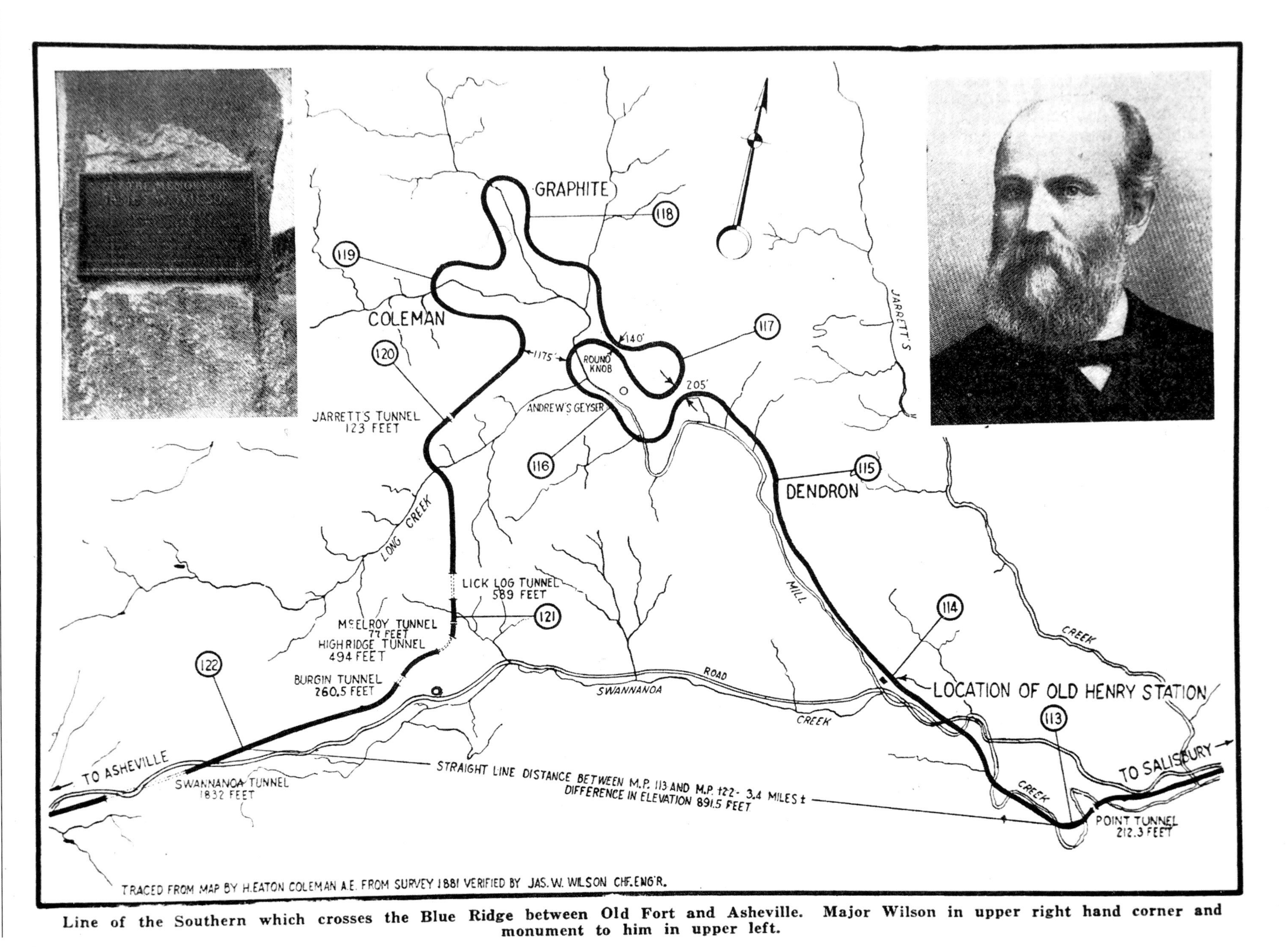


**Line of the Southern which crosses the Blue Ridge between Old Fort and Asheville. Major Wilson in upper right hand corner and monument to him in upper left.**

The sheer essence, the absolute thrill, the most dramatic exhibition of mountain railroading in the steam era can be found in this photo. It is a scene that cannot be adequately described into words. Just look at this most exhilarating exposure and allow your imagination to do the rest!

Here we have a massive, powerful 2-10-2, which was shown obviously working upgrade since the angle of the grade was clearly depicted in this photo, blasting its way westward. The engineer had his throttle wide-opened and his sanders working while his fireman had his stoker on to make sure the "big girl" kept its steam pressure at 200 lbs., so that it could use every bit of its 74,000 lbs. of tractive effort in order to get the tonnage dragging behind its huge tender to Asheville.

No. 5059 is showing near the siding at Dendron, N. C., above the area known as the "Cinder Fill" (milepost 115 on the map) with 1st No. 51, a through freight, at near 15 m.p.h. this afternoon in Nov. of 1947.

Can you imagine being this photographer, hearing one of the Southern's most powerful locomotives, "down on its knees," several minutes before it crawled into view. He not only heard No. 5059's struggle but could also see its massive plume of smoke shooting skyward, getting nearer and nearer. Then, from around the curve, the 2-10-2 slowly approaches. Now he understood why the "shotgunning," the huge volume of smoke and increasing tremble of the ground was all necessary!

This sight was so dramatic, so captivating, surely the "gods of railroading" stopped whatever they were doing in order to watch this glorious spectacle! This was truly mountain railroading personified!

*Credit: Photographer, Wayne Brumbaugh; Curt Tillotson Collection.*

No. 5025 (Ss-class 2-10-2): drivers: 57"; engine weight: 367,000 lbs.; steam pressure: 200 lbs.; tractive effort: 73,600 lbs.; superheated; Baldwin built:1917; tender weight (loaded with 9,000 gal. of water and 12 tons of coal): 171,000 lbs.; engine & tender length: 84'3 1/2"; engine height: 15'3"; Franklin lateral motion driving boxes on front axles; Cole trailing trucks; retired:Dec. of 1951.

When a train approached a tunnel-especially a steam powered freight-the engineer would ease off his throttle for two reasons: by not producing large quantities of smoke, it would not fill the cab making it hot, hard to see and breathe, plus by not working full throttle, you would not damage the tunnel's roof. However, once the engine cleared the bore, the engineer would pull the throttle all the way back on the quadrant, open his sanders while the fireman turned on his stoker-all producing a most captivating scene with a pandemonium of incredible sounds, smoke shooting skyward like an eruption of a small volcano and creating a moment in rail history that once seen and heard would remain with you throughout the remainder of your life.

This "fire breathing, smoke spewing," massive Southern Ss-class 2-10-2, No. 5025, is shown just out of the short Jarrett Tunnel and approaching an area known by railroaders as "Moore Cut,"

Believe it or not, within 10-15 minutes this struggling westbound extra freight, headed by Southern's powerful Ss-class, Richmond-built (1918) 2-10-2, No. 5079, will have its train on the tracks that appear on the hill in the top left corner of this photo! I can support this "phenomenon" since I rode the "Carolina Special" (No. 21) over this portion of the Asheville Division's Salisbury-Asheville line. And I was totally amazed when the conductor of this grand old train whose name was steeped in rail history, told me to look up to the hill on the right side of my train: "We'll be up there in a few minutes and then you can look down on the tracks we're on right now." He was correct!

In order to keep the grades under 2%, the engineers who pushed this route through the Blue Ridge Mountains to Asheville, the "Land of the Sky," had to travel 12 miles of curves, deep fills and 7 tunnels in order to reach Ridgecrest, N. C.-3.4 miles from Old Fort to Ridgecrest in a straight line. It was (and remains) an engineering marvel.

Extra 5079 West is shown passing the strategic Dendron, N. C. pass track (116 miles from Salisbury) on this automatic block protected, busy mountain railroad at approximately 2:00 p.m. this cold afternoon in Feb. of 1947, pulling 30 cars with its caboose seen to the right of this photo. No. 5079 was shooting a plume of smoke skyward (most of which was condensation-the white part-which happened when hot exhaust met the cold mountain air). Soon, however, the smoke would be all black as the fireman would turn on his stoker in order to keep the engine filled with the required 200 lbs. of steam so that the 2-10-2 could use all of its 74,000 lbs. of tractive effort to get its train to the tracks above it. As a result, the photographer had an opportunity to photograph this extra west (with its white flags still white!) not only at its current location, he could also make an additional exposure of the same train running from left to right on the big hill above his current position!

Man, it does not get much better than this! Hearing the "shotgunning" of No. 5079 for over 30 minutes was wonderful. And just think, only the crews of Norfolk Southern trains can witness these wondrous sights today since no passenger service exists on the "Swannanoa Route."

*Credit: Photographer, Wayne Brumbaugh; Curt Tillotson Collection.*

after passing through Coleman, N. C. (milepost 120 on the map) with the hard working westbound 3rd No. 51, bound for Asheville, N. C. this cold afternoon in Feb. of 1947.

Because of the numerous grades west of Old Fort, N. C., the 2-10-2's were the standard road power on a vast majority of both west and eastbound freights. The 73,600 lbs. of tractive effort of No. 5025 was needed to keep the tonnage moving. And in order to negotiate the many curves-some quite sharp-the 2-10-2's, as well as the 4-8-2 passenger power, had Franklin lateral motion driving boxes placed on the first set of driver, enabling them to move, somewhat, into the curves without remaining rigid. As a result, the wear and tear on the driver flanges and track was reduced considerably.

This was another photo depicting an event that had to be seen and heard to fully appreciate just what was happening right in front of this photographer, who must have had a big smile on his face while looking through his camera's viewfinder as he released his shutter and recorded another example of mountain railroading at its thrilling best!

*Credit: Photographer, Wayne Brumbaugh; Curt Tillotson Collection.*

No. 5064 (Ss-class 2-10-2): drivers: 57: engine weight: 378,000 lbs.; steam pressure: 200 lbs.; tractive effort: 74,000 lbs.; superheated; Richmond built:1918; tender weight (loaded with 9,000 gal. of water and 12 tons of coal): 171,000 lbs.; engine & tender length: 84'8"; engine height: 15'3"; Cole trailer trucks; Franklin lateral motion driver boxes placed on its first set of driver axles; retired: April of 1952.

When I first looked at this excellent photo, three things caught my eyes, other than that massive Southern Ss-class 2-10-2, No. 5064, blasting its way west toward Asheville, N. C. with freight No. 51 in May of 1949.

First, the sight of this huge Santa Fe type steamer passing through Point Tunnel-just west of Old Fort-at milepost 113. Notice there was no smoke in the tunnel. When possible, an engineer would gather as much momentum as he could when approaching a tunnel. Then he would cut off his throttle and coast through the bore, thereby avoiding all that smoke coming into his cab. Once in the open, the "hogger" would pull his throttle way back on its quadrant to keep his tonnage moving.

The second thing that drew my attention was the fact that No. 5064 had just crossed over a short bridge and entered one of the many sharp curves found between Old Fort and Ridgecrest on the Southern's busy Salisbury-Asheville line. These sharp curves caused the Southern to install Franklin lateral motion driving boxes on the front set of drivers of this long engine-base "hog," so as to reduce the wear of its driver flanges and damage to the track. This device was installed in the 4-8-2 passenger power as well.

Finally, I spotted an object that you cannot find anymore. No. 5064 is shown "shotgunning" under "tell tails." During the steam era, a brakeman might ride or walk on top of the cars while in motion. When approaching tunnels, bridges, overpasses or any other low lying obstructions that came close to the top of the train, the railroad installed "tell tails"-look at the pole on the right of the 2-10-2 which anchored a horizontal bar high above the track from which several sections of rope dangled down. If the brakeman was unaware of an approaching low obstruction, he would be gently hit by these strands of rope which would warn him to DUCK! Today's railroad equipment, in general, do not have "catwalks" on top of the cars, so all "tell tails" have been removed.

These examples give you a reason to look at the entire photo. Of course, the engine and train would be the first thing to draw your (and my) attention. Still, after looking at the magnificent action, inspect the rest of the photo. You might find something interesting.

Still, just look at that big, burly Richmond built 2-10-2, moving through freight No. 51, creating a scene of mountain railroading at its best!

*Credit: Photographer Unknown; Curt Tillotson Collection.*

No. 5059 (Ss-class 2-10-2): drivers: 57" engine weight: 378,000 lbs.; steam pressure: 200 lbs.; Richmond built: 1918; tender weight (loaded with 9,000 gal. of water and 12 tons of coal): 171,000 lbs.; engine & tender length: 84'8"; engine height: 15'3"; Franklin lateral motion driving boxes on the front pair of drivers; Cole trailer trucks; retired: July of 1952; pusher engine, No. 5052.

When an extra long and/or heavy freight from Salisbury, N. C. arrived in Old Fort, N. C., there were two options, during the

No. 5052 (Ss-class 2-10-2-"pusher" engine): drivers: 57"; engine weight: 367,000 lbs.; steam pressure: 200 lbs.; tractive effort: 73,600 lbs.; superheated; Baldwin built: 1918; tender weight (loaded with 9,000 gal. of water and 12 tons of coal): 171,000 lbs.; engine & tender length: 84'3 1/2"; engine height: 15'3"; Franklin lateral motion driving boxes on the front pair of drivers; Cole trailer trucks; retired: Dec. of 1951; *No. 5059-road engine.*

After the photographer recorded the passage of Southern's mighty Ss-class 2-10-2, No. 5059, pulling an extra freight westbound near Dendron, N. C. this particular afternoon in Aug. of 1947, he heard another, hard-working, massive 2-10-2 getting closer to his location at milepost No. 115 on the road's Salisbury to Asheville line. He knew that with the route being protected by automatic block signals, another train could not be following the extra 5059 West that close. As a result, it could only be one thing, the extra west had a "friend" on its rear end in order to help it battle the grades, curves and tunnels on the 12 miles of scenic but treacherous mountain railroading between Old Fort and Ridgecrest, N. C. He was correct!

Within minutes that loud "talking Leviathan" appeared and the photographer captured another example of "normal" mountain railroading when 2-10-2, No. 5052, whose fireman still had his stoker on, came into view with a large volume of smoke rolling out of the stack.

The conductor of the extra west, along with the rear end brakeman, received an up-close and personal experience of hearing the "shotgunning" of No. 5052 as the huge "hog" worked up the stiff grade, preparing to uncouple the helper from his caboose "on the fly" so Extra 5059 could continue its struggle to Asheville.

This was actually a normal procedure in the mountains; however, to a "flatlander" such as yours truly, it was a fascinating experience-one not forgotten!

*Credit: Photographer Unknown; Curt Tillotson Collection.*

steam era, on how to get the tonnage over the next 12 miles toward Asheville, N. C. Those 12 miles involved grades, sharp curves, tunnels and other obstacles that the Blue Ridge Mountains had in store for freight and passenger trains that had to venture into those beautiful "challenges."

One of those procedures involved the following movements: the train could "double" the 12 miles, i.e., move half of the train to Ridgecrest, N. C., leaving them there, then the engine would return to Old Fort, get the remaining cars to Ridgecrest, re-assemble the entire train and then continue its journey to Asheville. The remaining option-the one that was preferred-would involve adding an additional 2-10-2 to the rear of the train and then, with the crews coordinating their movements over the hills and through the tunnels, it was like watching actors in a play-without radio communication! The engine crews were that good.

Extra 5059 West used option No. 2. On the point of the westbounder was Southern's Ss-class 2-10-2, No. 5059, using all of its 74,000 lbs. of tractive effort to move the train upgrade (notice how the rear cars seem to drop off downhill) near Dendron, N. C. (milepost 115 on your map) with the sand of thousands of similar movements almost up to the top of the rails.

Meanwhile, 50+ cars to the rear was a sister 2-10-2, No. 5052, using all of its 74,000 lbs. of t.e. in pushing the tonnage as hard as its 57" drivers could manage. The engine crews were communicating through whistle "talk" and air pressure readings plus that all-important "experience."

A train powered by two engines was a fascinating sight to see and hear and, especially, to photograph. Hearing one massive 2-10-2 "cannonading" with all its might, having these sounds echoing off the mountains was one thing; having two 2-10-2's "shotgunning," was almost too much for you to comprehend unless you were there, in person. Since this is impossible for you and I, our only option is to look at the photo and use our imagination and try to duplicate what the photographer must have experienced.

*Credit: Photographer Unknown; Curt Tillotson Collection.*

No.5046 (Ss-class 2-10-2): drivers: 57"; engine weight: 378,000 lbs.; steam pressure: 200 lbs.; tractive effort: 74,000 lbs.; superheated; Richmond built: 1918; tender weight (loaded with 9,000 gal. of water and 12 tons of coal): 171,000 lbs.; engine & tender length:84'8"; engine height:15'3"; Franklin lateral motion driving boxes on front driver axles; Cole trailer trucks; retired: April of 1952, *meeting No. 15, the "Asheville Special"*.

Here is a railfan's dream come true. We have steam power in action in the mountains plus a "meet" between two trains with both pulled by steam locomotives. This was not just an ordinary meet, however, for a 2-10-2 powered eastbound freight (shown "in the hole") was meeting a green and gold colored 4-8-2 hustling a westbound passenger train-Southern's No. 15, the "Asheville Special"-near Coleman, N. C. (m.p. 119) on a cloudy morning in May of 1948. Like I said: this was truly a railfan's dream that actually came true, at least for this photographer, and due to his luck, for you and I as well.

Through freight No. 52, headed by Ss-class No. 5064, is shown moving slowly through this pass track, heading for the spring switch at the east end of the siding, while the big and beautiful, green and gold colored Ts-1 class No. 1476, pulling 9 cars of No. 15 without a helper engine, "blasted" by at a 25-30 m.p.h. pace on its way to Asheville. No. 15 departed New York City at 1:30 p.m. the day before; it pulled out of Greensboro, N. C.-and the Washington-Atlanta main line-at 2:30 a.m. and would arrive in the "Land of the Sky" (Asheville) by 9:00 a.m. No. 52 should arrive in Spencer Yard between 11:00 a.m. and 12:00 p.m.

I have found that you have far more locations to make your exposures during the late fall, winter and early spring seasons since the summer period-with all the leaves on the trees, the tremendous amount of brush and undergrowth plus snakes-made many areas almost inaccessible. However, I must admit that the summer growth helps to make your photos more scenic on occasions.

Speaking of the spring switches, because of them No. 52 would be able to re-enter the main line without having to stop, open the switch, pull out onto the main and have the caboose crew close the switch. It was a time saver.

THIS was mountain railroading that you and I wish we could experience firsthand. As a result, we are thankful for the photographer who recorded this drama which helps us realize what it must have been like seeing such wondrous events which occurred on a daily basis: GREAT!

*Credit: Photographer, Frank Clodfelter; Curt Tillotson Collection.*

Of all the divisions on the Southern, the Asheville Division, whose engines had to face the mountains each and every day, regardless of what direction they were heading, accumulating all the smoke, sanding, grease and the usual road grime, always seemed to have more white colors on their locomotive pony trucks and driver rims; more graphite on their smoke boxes and stacks; cleaner engine jackets and tender sides; shiny bells, plus their operational abilities were always at their best, regardless of the engine size or class: this included elegant green and gold colored 4-8-2's; the powerful 2-10-2's; the massive 2-8-8-2's; and even their Consolidations, Mikados and switchers on this proud division. The crews even had their engines washed almost after every run.

This photo gives the railfans an idea of this pride the Asheville Division crews had for "their" engines. This eastbound local freight, powered by No. 871, a Ks-1 class 2-8-0, is shown working up a slight grade, approaching Jarretts Tunnel (milepost 120.6-from Salisbury, N. C.) in a style that would rival that of a far more powerful 2-10-2, with its smoke shooting into a magnificent sky (what I call a "photographer's sky," with a few clouds to fill up that void of blank sky). No. 871 (built in 1906) was performing as efficiently and as dramatically as any other mountain power this beautiful afternoon in July of 1940, even though it was 34 years old.

Yes, even in the mountains where Southern engines required far more "exertions" than their counterparts in flatter terrain, their engines were exceptionally attractive and remained so, run after run. And even up to the arrival of the diesels, you could still identify what division the locomotive had been assigned: the Danville, Charlotte, Washington, etc., but especially those from the Asheville Division.

No. 871 (Ks-1 class 2-8-0): drivers: 57"; engine weight: 205,000 lbs.; steam pressure: 200 lbs.; tractive effort: 44,081 lbs.; Baldwin built: 1906; tender weight (loaded with 7,500 gal. of water and 12 tons of coal): 146,380 lbs.; engine & tender length: 56'9"; engine height, 15'1 1/4"; retired: March of 1950.

Before the 1982 merger with the Norfolk & Western, which created the current Norfolk Southern, the Southern had a well-deserved reputation of possessing one of the most esthetically pleasing and efficient fleet of motive power-especially their steam locomotives-in the rail world. In fact, each division of the road took great pride in the care of their "iron horses." Indeed, during the 1930's and 1940's, one could almost always tell what division a locomotive was assigned by just its appearance!

*Photographer, Frank Clodfelter; Curt Tillotson Collection.*

# Bibliography

Banks, Harold and Shelby F. Lowe. SOUTHERN STEAM POWER. Omaha: Barnhart Press, 1966.

Bryant, H. Stafford, Jr., THE GEORGIAN LOCOMOTIVE. Barre, Mass.: Barre Gazzette, 1962.

Burke, Davis. THE SOUTHERN RAILWAY. Chapel Hill, N. C.: University of North Carolina Press, 1985.

Gilbert, John F. CROSSTIES OVER SALUDA. Raleigh, N. C.: The Crossties Press, 1982.

Prince, Richard E. SOUTHERN RAILWAY SYSTEM STEAM LOCOMOTIVES AND BOATS. Green River, Wyo.: Richard Prince, 1970.

RAILROAD Magazine. “Southern Steam Power.” Kokomo, Ind.: Popular Publication, Vol, 51, No. 2, pp. 104-109. March, 1950.

Tillotson, Curt C., Jr. CLASSIC STEAM TRAINS OF THE SOUTH. Lynchburg, Va.: TLC Publishing, Inc., 2000.

*See Page 91 in "Mighty Saluda Grade"*

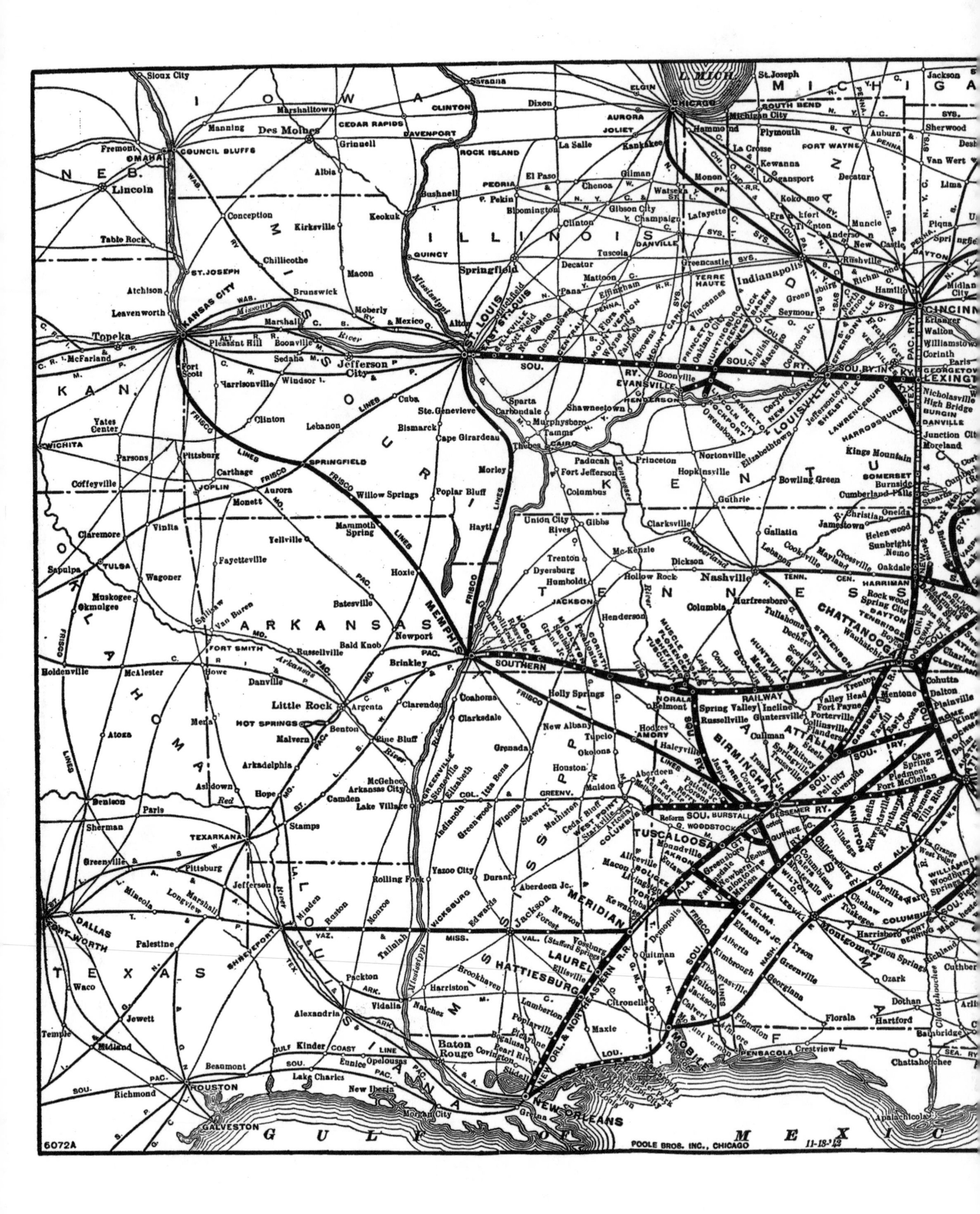

IOWA
NEB.
KAN.
MISSOURI
ILLINOIS
INDIANA
MICHIGAN
KENTUCKY
TENNESSEE
ARKANSAS
OKLAHOMA
TEXAS
LOUISIANA
MISSISSIPPI
ALABAMA
FLA.
GULF OF MEXICO
L. MICH.
Sioux City
Savanna
Marshalltown
CLINTON
CEDAR RAPIDS
DAVENPORT
ROCK ISLAND
Des Moines
Grinnell
Manning
Fremont
OMAHA
COUNCIL BLUFFS
Lincoln
Albia
Conception
Kirksville
Keokuk
Bushnell
QUINCY
Table Rock
Chillicothe
Macon
ST. JOSEPH
Atchison
Brunswick
KANSAS CITY
Leavenworth
Topeka
McFarland
Marshall
Moberly
Mexico
Boonville
Pleasant Hill
Sedalia
Jefferson City
Fort Scott
Harrisonville
Windsor
Clinton
Yates Center
Wichita
Parsons
Pittsburg
Carthage
Joplin
Coffeyville
Monett
Aurora
Springfield
SPRINGFIELD
FRISCO LINES
Lebanon
Cuba
ST. LOUIS
EAST ST. LOUIS
Alton
Ste. Genevieve
Bismarck
Cape Girardeau
Willow Springs
Poplar Bluff
Morley
Hayti
Mammoth Spring
Yellville
Claremore
Vinita
Sapulpa
TULSA
Muskogee
Okmulgee
Wagoner
Fayetteville
Van Buren
FORT SMITH
Russellville
Batesville
Hoxie
Bald Knob
Newport
MEMPHIS
Brinkley
Holdenville
McAlester
Howe
Danville
Little Rock
Argenta
Clarendon
HOT SPRINGS
Benton
Malvern
Pine Bluff
Mena
Atoka
Arkadelphia
Ashdown
Hope
Camden
McGehee
Arkansas City
Lake Village
Denison
Paris
Sherman
TEXARKANA
Stamps
Greenville
Pittsburg
Jefferson
Marshall
Longview
Mineola
DALLAS
FORT WORTH
Palestine
SHREVEPORT
Minden
Ruston
Monroe
VICKSBURG
Tallulah
Waco
Jewett
Temple
Midland
Beaumont
HOUSTON
Richmond
GALVESTON
Kinder
Lake Charles
New Iberia
Morgan City
Opelousas
Eunice
Alexandria
Packton
Vidalia
Natchez
Harriston
Baton Rouge
Covington
Slidell
NEW ORLEANS
Gretna
Brookhaven
HATTIESBURG
LAUREL
Ellisville
MERIDIAN
Jackson
Newton
Forest
Edwards
Yazoo City
Rolling Fork
Durant
Greenwood
Indianola
Winona
Grenada
Clarksdale
Coahoma
Holly Springs
New Albany
Tupelo
Okolona
Houston
Aberdeen
Amory
WEST POINT
Starkville
COLUMBUS
Corinth
Jackson
Humboldt
Dyersburg
Trenton
Union City
McKenzie
Hollow Rock
Henderson
Nashville
Murfreesboro
Columbia
Tullahoma
Dickson
Clarksville
Gallatin
Lebanon
Cookeville
CHATTANOOGA
DAYTON
HARRIMAN
Oakdale
Crossville
Jamestown
Oneida
Helenwood
Knoxville
Cleveland
Cohutta
Dalton
Stevenson
Decherd
Scottsboro
Guntersville
Cullman
BIRMINGHAM
Bessemer
Anniston
Talladega
Gadsden
Attalla
TUSCALOOSA
Greensboro
Marion
SELMA
Montgomery
Greenville
Georgiana
Tyson
Opelika
Auburn
Tuskegee
COLUMBUS
Union Springs
Ozark
Dothan
Florala
Hartford
Chattahoochee
Crestview
PENSACOLA
MOBILE
Mount Vernon
Citronelle
Quitman
Demopolis
Livingston
York
Eutaw
Akron
Mooresville
Apalachicola
Bainbridge
Louisville
LOUISVILLE
LEXINGTON
Frankfort
CINCINNATI
Hamilton
Dayton
Richmond
Indianapolis
Terre Haute
Vincennes
Evansville
Henderson
Owensboro
Paducah
Cairo
Thebes
Tamms
Carbondale
Murphysboro
Sparta
Shawneetown
Princeton
Hopkinsville
Bowling Green
Elizabethtown
Nicholasville
High Bridge
Danville
Junction City
Somerset
Burnside
Paris
Corinth
Williamstown
Walton
Erlanger
Georgetown
Springfield
Decatur
Mattoon
Effingham
Pana
Tuscola
Champaign
Danville
Bloomington
Peoria
El Paso
Pekin
Chenoa
Gilman
Kankakee
La Salle
Dixon
CHICAGO
ELGIN
AURORA
JOLIET
Hammond
Michigan City
SOUTH BEND
St. Joseph
Plymouth
La Crosse
Kewanna
Logansport
Monon
Lafayette
Kokomo
Frankfort
Anderson
Muncie
New Castle
Rushville
FORT WAYNE
Auburn
Decatur
Lima
Piqua
Van Wert
Sherwood
Jackson
Greencastle
Seymour
North Vernon
Madison
Oakland City
Princeton
Cumberland Falls
Kings Mountain
SOUTHERN
SOU. RY.
RAILWAY
SOUTHERN RAILWAY
NEW ORL. & NORTHEASTERN R.R.
Mississippi
Missouri
Arkansas
Red
River
Tennessee
Cumberland
6072A
POOLE BROS. INC., CHICAGO
11-18-'12